Tucson's M

A Collection of Ghostly Tales from the Old Pueblo

Katie Mullaly and J. Patrick Ohlde

Photography by Mikal Mullaly

Schiffer Publishing Ltd

4880 Lower Valley Road, Atglen, Pennsylvania 19310

Other Schiffer Books by Katie Mullaly & J. Patrick Ohlde
Scare-Izona: A Travel Guide to Arizona's Spookiest Spots, 978-0-7643-2844-2, $14.95

Other Schiffer Books on Related Subjects
Santa Fe Ghosts: Mystery, History, & Truth, 978-0-7643-3175-6, $14.99
Santa Fe & Taos: A History in Postcards, 0-7643-2384-9, $24.95
A Journey through Northern Arizona, 978-0-7643-3010-0, $24.99

Schiffer Books are available at special discounts for bulk purchases for sales promotions or premiums. Special editions, including personalized covers, corporate imprints, and excerpts can be created in large quantities for special needs. For more information contact the publisher:

Published by Schiffer Publishing Ltd.
4880 Lower Valley Road
Atglen, PA 19310
Phone: (610) 593-1777; Fax: (610) 593-2002
E-mail: Info@schifferbooks.com

For the largest selection of fine reference books on this and related subjects, please visit our web site at: **www.schifferbooks.com** We are always looking for people to write books on new and related subjects. If you have an idea for a book please contact us at the above address.

This book may be purchased from the publisher. Include $5.00 for shipping. Please try your bookstore first. You may write for a free catalog.

In Europe, Schiffer books are distributed by
Bushwood Books
6 Marksbury Ave.
Kew Gardens
Surrey TW9 4JF England
Phone: 44 (0) 20 8392-8585; Fax: 44 (0) 20 8392-9876
E-mail: info@bushwoodbooks.co.uk
Website: www.bushwoodbooks.co.uk
Free postage in the U.K., Europe; air mail at cost.

Designed by Stephanie Daugherty
Type set in Bard/NewsGoth BT

ISBN: 978-0-7643-3153-4
Printed in in the United States of America

Dedications

Katie dedicates this book to her husband Mikal, and her children, Seamus and Liam, who are, and forever will be, her reason for living.

Patrick wishes to dedicate this book to Peyton; "No matter what anyone else says, I will always love you, Buddy."

Acknowledgments

God – For providing an afterlife in the first place;

Mikal Mullaly – For being helpful and wonderful and an all-around good guy, and also for taking all the pictures in this book and *Scare-Izona* (for which we neglected to give him a specific credit);

Seamus and Liam – For being the best kids in the world, bar none;

Peyton – For, coincidentally, also being the best kid in the world, bar none;

Hazel Redmon – For telling everyone who would listen about her grandson the writer (even at the doctor's office)! Oh, and also for the trips to Red Lobster;

Lyle and Belinda Ohlde – For being the best parents in the world and never failing to be supportive;

Leslie and Felicia – For being excited about this whole writing business;

Kim and Jack Alfred – Because you thought you'd never be thanked in a book again;

Dan Bruns – For teaching Patrick to be a farmer;

Gabi Andres – For being able to do everything, all at once, girlfriend;

‡‡‡‡‡‡‡‡‡‡‡‡‡‡ Acknowledgements ‡‡‡‡‡‡‡‡‡‡‡‡‡‡

Linda and Mick; and Andrea and Corey – For enthusiastically contributing, and Corey, for not being too mad about his name being misspelled in the first book. (This acknowledgment is brought to you by the letter "E.");

Nicole Perdue – I spelled it right this time!

Chris Ouillette – For support, leads, and enthusiasm;

Summer Disney – For helping with interview questions and tasty cupcakes;

Veronica Morrison – For supporting all the goofy media stuff that Patrick does;

Jaci Vigil – For her outstanding editing prowess;

Ross Bowns – For blazing an artistic trail to success;

Steve Ramirez – For getting that yearbook!

Dinah Roseberry and everyone at Schiffer Publishing – For liking our books well enough to print them;

Robin, Liza, and Jasmine – For letting us investigate at all hours of the day and night, and for putting up with all those ghosts;

William Everist – For teaching us everything we know about ghosts;

The Noble Platypus – For proving that anything is possible;

Special Thanks Goes To...

We send special notes of acknowledgment to Maureen, Christopher, Ian, Cheryl, Justin, Lee, Teddy, and Wyatt; John, Teresa, Sean Patrick, Cherie, Kayla, and Brian; Diane; Zack Alfred; Dan Wallace; Jeff Stephenson; Troy Haag; Jose Solis (for serving his country proudly); Dan, Jenny, Davin, and Nathan; Mark Ghio; and Justin Cunningham.

We would also like to acknowledge the following people for their contributions: Desiree, Mila, Randy, Cricket, Cassandra and William, Judy Ciampoli, Michelle, Melissa and Ray, Kat, Ron, Shannon, Julia Benites Arriola at Sosa-Carrillo-Fremont House, Terry Hogsett at Tom's Furniture, Joey and Cecelia at Wooden Nickel Tavern, Belinda and Andrew, The Hill family at Z Mansion, Sarah, Frances Causey at Old Tucson, Anne, Bobby, DJ, Tiffany, and Sammy, Gertrude from Copper Bell, Patches, Goldie, and Rowdy.

Contents

‡‡‡‡‡‡‡‡‡‡‡‡‡‡‡‡‡ Contents ‡‡‡‡‡‡‡‡‡‡‡‡‡‡‡‡‡‡

Introduction

The number one most consistent thing you are asked as a paranormal investigator is, "Am I crazy?" Probably the second most consistent would be, "Are you crazy?" Generally the answer to both questions is an unqualified "no." It is the misunderstanding of the paranormal and its rampant misrepresentation through various media channels that lead to the questions being asked in the first place. It is with that in mind that we set out to write this book.

There are as many beliefs and theories surrounding survival after death as there are people to hold them. It makes sense too, given that it's in our best interest as people to be able to continue on after death. All of the world's religions deal in some way or another with this idea, be it a belief in a heaven and hell to a more pessimistic view that there is no afterlife. Somewhere mixed in that great debate there is the study of the paranormal. For most people, the closest brush with the paranormal they will have is through various and sundry media. Movies, TV shows, and books are chock-full of the paranormal and run the gamut from the realistic to the ridiculous. Some shows will look and act real but still be a fabrication, some will be cleverly disguised commercials for home maintenance services, and some will be accurate accounts of the paranormal. Then there is all of the outright fiction. The paranormal is the horror writer's bread and butter as they weave tales of ghosts, psychic abilities, and all that it implies. The field is wide open for interpretation and fantasy, but what if you want to know for sure? What if you want to know what it's really like to have a brush with the paranormal? That is what we are dealing with here.

In the world of paranormal investigation, much like in media, there are different takes on what is real and what is not. Some people investigate from the hip, some from study, and some from your pocketbook. There are those who have gained their training from their religious beliefs and some from science, some from intuition, and some from upbringing. Some will even be constructing their views out of whole cloth with the clear and singular intention of separating you from your hard-earned dollars. Reading that list you may have noticed that I mentioned that last group twice. That isn't an error, but rather an indication that there are probably twice as many charlatans as there are legitimate researchers out there and when money for services rendered becomes an issue, that ratio jumps up rather steeply, but I'm getting ahead of myself.

The methodologies involved in an investigation are also varied and disparate between many groups as they utilize all of the aforementioned sources to draw from. Groups do things very differently and often that can both determine and be determined by their particular intentions. There are those groups who are out to prove to the world once and for all that ghosts are real, and even those are split into their own subsets; those being groups who are governed by strict scientific methods and those who mean well, but don't have the training and knowledge of those scientific methods. Then there are people who are doing it purely for fun. Perhaps they might like the idea of it, or are into horror movies and thrill rides. Others are doing it for a living, operating like an exterminator or plumber, showing up to look into your pipes, trying to fix your problem, and then presenting you with a big, fat bill. And again, some of them are trying to make their living by impinging on yours, or more specifically your beliefs in the surviving dead.

It's impossible to say that one way is right and the other method is wrong unless there is a particular stated goal. If you're looking to do publishable scientific work fit to change the minds of the skeptics, then you really need to know your equipment, statistical analysis, and general methodologies. If you just want to have fun with your friends, then you're good to go in whatever manner you see fit—as long as it isn't illegal, disrespectful, or unethical. Just what separates good clean fun from the bad, "lands you in jail with a heap of guilty conscience" fun will be left to the reader's discretion. The point is that your intentions count for a lot when you're an investigator...as they affect every aspect of your investigation from top to bottom.

However you do it though, one thing that tends to be consistent amongst groups is that often the locations they investigate are public places like hotels, theaters, restaurants, Civil War battlegrounds, cemeteries, and the occasional toy store. The reasons for this are fairly obvious: public places are the easiest to get into, they are often known to be haunted, and the stories are more readily available for verification. It's just easier and more convenient, and frankly, if you are an amateur group getting started, these places may be your only options.

There is certainly nothing at all wrong with this. Intention is everything and if you intend to go investigate a haunted place, then going to a known public haunted place is good business. It is obviously pointless to go to a place that is not haunted and try to scare up some ghosts. So, the well-known public sites are not bad ideas and will serve you well. Indeed, even the documentaries about haunted places that grace basic cable channels will give you a look into these sorts of public places. Often, they can get into places that your garden-variety investigators won't manage—like decommissioned and closed-down mental hospitals or top-tier private residences and tourist attractions. As we discovered during the writing of our previous book, you sometimes need credentials from a cable channel to get into well-known tourist locations without paying an exorbitant fee. The fact that said location may have to have its "ghosties" on its payroll in order to guarantee desired results is neither here nor there.

But what you don't hear about so often are the everyday ghost stories that regular people have to tell. You don't hear about the stories coming from people with nothing to sell and nothing to gain and are really quite distressed and freaked out about the activity. You don't hear about the lady unable to sleep because of noises in the house or children too scared to turn off the light at night for fear of the shapes that move around in the dark. You don't hear about any of the less sensational — but absolutely terrifying — events that occur to everyday people, well, every day.

These stories aren't the easiest to come by either. Sure, when you are standing around the office talking with your co-workers at Halloween time, someone will let slip that a neighbor of theirs sees a ghost or their buddy lives in a house where things move around of their own accord. You hear about the people they know like some urban legend passed on in an ever-changing game of telephone where details are dropped or enhanced and it becomes the plot of a Wes Craven movie before it's done. Of course, the sources of these stories play them close to their chests for fear of an affirmative answer to the first question posed in this introduction. They tell these stories in hushed confidences, always beginning with the caveat, "I swear I am not crazy" or "You are going to think this is totally nuts." It is that sort of story we want to embrace in this book. We have scoured Tucson, Arizona, for these everyday stories, these street-level, in-the-trenches stories that are often much more chilling than their well-known counterparts, mostly because they don't stop when you turn in your room key the next morning. They are terrifying because for these people, it represents their daily life, and going through life, *everyday*, being afraid of things they don't understand — as well as the possibility that these things are nothing more than a symptom of a condition that requires intense psychological counseling — creates an existence centered on oppression and strict secrecy. Because of this, these stories seem much more real and much more tangible because they aren't happening to someone else, someone professionally trained to investigate... *they are happening to people just like you.*

It's important to feature these stories for a couple of reasons; first, they are undiluted by commercialism. This is not to say that public places are going to try to bilk you or lure you in with promises of all manner of paranormal shenanigans. Indeed, not one of the locations covered in our first book was looking for publicity regarding their activity, and they were very kind to let us come in and investigate. Still, there are some locations, such as the previously mentioned landmark, that may be sub-contracting their haunting activity, that try to bend the collected data to the conclusion they are looking for rather than come to some reasonable conclusion based on the data collected. There is a really big difference here. Because the people in haunted houses want to not be crazy, they would just as soon have the activity stop outright or be some easily fixed plumbing problem than to have to live in a haunted house. In these instances, it becomes much easier to believe reports of activity in the home. Of course, that's not to say that public hauntings are not credible; it simply illustrates that stories involving private homes are typically more of the front-line variety. The people telling the stories are the people they happened to and are thus a bit more personal and specific.

Second, and this is the more altruistic of the reasons, is that people who live with haunting activity routinely feel crazy and are reluctant to talk about their experiences because they're afraid of being judged. Indeed, in any sort of vacuum, one feels like his particular experience sets him apart from everyone else and this fear of being different or being seen as different tends to alienate. So the goal then becomes "how do I best hide from everyone else the fact that I am a freak?" Obviously, this is an unhealthy way to go about life. Alienation from the collective tends to color every aspect of your life and that separation, or separateness as it feels, can be potentially damaging to all areas of a person's life, leading to isolation and avoidance of human contact and ultimately whittle a person down to a husk of an existence in which he feels like he can never talk to anyone for fear of exposure. Clearly this is a worst-case scenario as most people who experience this just don't talk about it to others and get quiet when the subject is brought up. Still, when it happens, it's always there in the back of your mind that there's something wrong with you. In delivering these stories, we hope to demonstrate, in no uncertain terms, there is NOTHING wrong with you and there are plenty of people who go through the same thing every day. By this, I don't mean weirdoes in fedoras and trenchcoats running about with crystals talking about vortexes of energy; no, I'm talking about regular everyday people who go to work, pay their taxes, watch "Desperate Housewives" ... *and also live with a ghost*. These people are not alone and we want to make sure they know that. If you're one of those people, relax and get comfortable because you're amongst friends here. If you're not one of those people, I would advise you to take heed anyway because you never know when you might become one.

What Are Ghosts?

If you live on this planet and watch TV or go to the movies, especially around Halloween, you're going to form some sort of notion about ghosts and hauntings and, sadly, through no fault of your own, it will most likely be the wrong one. As mentioned earlier, the media loves ghosts, but it does not always love accuracy. Indeed, when focusing on entertainment, it's easy to see how someone wanting to fill theater seats or increase their ratings would embellish or fabricate out of whole cloth. Again, there is nothing at all wrong with that. The entertainment industry is under no obligation whatsoever to provide truth and, in fact, it's often quite the opposite. Still, an unfortunate side effect of this for people who are involved with the paranormal is that there is an ungodly amount of misinformation out there. Add to that people who can't be bothered to research anything and would rather just make it up, and you have a very convoluted and confusing field. It's no wonder that skeptics and atheists have such an easy time with us; we are running around haphazard in disparate directions and with an infinite number of explanations for what a ghost or haunting is, or the paranormal in general. It's with this in mind that we provide you with an easy-to-use primer clarifying terms and making clear the accepted scientific classifications.

But first, before even getting into the types of ghosts and activity there are, we would like to clarify that the topic of the paranormal, while often filed next to them in bookstores, does not include UFOs, aliens, or monsters. Anything regarding Area 51, the Grays, or Sasquatch is not covered under the paranormal umbrella. Each of these topics belong to its own category such as UFO-logy or crypto-zoology. The subject of the paranormal deals primarily with unexplained phenomena as it applies to humans. This would include extra-sensory perception (ESP), psychokinesis (PK), remote viewing, telepathy, and, yes, *ghosts*. There is certainly nothing wrong with any of the aforementioned similar subjects, but they just do not happen to fall specifically under the auspices of the paranormal.

So now that we have covered what the paranormal *is not*, let's get into what *it is* as it applies to ghosts and hauntings. You will hear about a wide variety of activity in the stories that follow and it's not all the same. Not all ghosts are created equal and in many cases are not ghosts at all. With this sort of study, nothing is set in stone and there are no absolutes, but over time investigators have compiled some classifications for types of activity that tend to be consistent. As with anything in the field, we are talking about best guesses here, but with the accumulation of data over the years, it is a very good guess.

On the surface, the classification of ghost types seems pretty simple. There are only three of them after all, and how complicated can it be? Given the novel-length number of different answers that you get when requesting a definition for each of them, the answer is that it gets to be very complicated. The reason for this, for the most part, is that the terms can get a bit confusing because they are often applied to more than one type of activity or used interchangeably with each other. This is exacerbated when people don't take the time to clarify, so we will take this opportunity to belabor the points.

Apparition: This is what most people think of when they think of ghosts. The apparition is literally the spirit of a dead person stuck on earth for some reason we don't know about. People will tell you it is traumatic death or unfinished business, and it may well be, but no one really knows for sure. That an apparition seems to display sentience only strengthens the above suppositions, but still, until you can ask a ghost directly, you aren't going to know for sure. Plenty of people claim to be able to talk to spirits and receive answers, but we remain skeptical of most of these claims as anything more than cold reading and chicanery. Despite this, apparitions do seem to respond to requests for them to leave you alone and that further suggests that there is some kind of intelligent thought going on in these cases.

Most people, if asked, would probably claim to have a pretty sturdy grasp on this classification, but the presentation of the apparition is where people usually go wrong. An apparition appears most often as a silhouette, white or black in color and often in the vague shape of a person. Sometimes, they will present as mist or a more indistinct shape, but they are most often person-shaped. Generally, when people see an apparition, they will see the figure out of their peripheral vision. Most people report that when they turn to look at the apparition, it disappears and they are left with that feeling you get when you walk down the hallway and pass some clothes hanging on a door and for a moment you think it's a person standing there, only to turn and see your grandmother's undergarments, or the devil mask your brother put there so you would see it and scream. Seeing an apparition is much like that only when you turn...you see nothing at all rather than a pair of drying knickers or a Halloween mask.

On the otherhand, if you are seeing a distinct image of someone with full human features and they are wearing clothing or holding objects, it is NOT an apparition. Since items of clothing and objects aren't commonly believed to have souls, there is no way for them to be represented on something that is made up of nothing but a spirit. The fashion industry has yet to get a foothold on the ethereal plane, and while your leather biker jacket sure looks cool, it's probably not cool enough to accompany you to the afterlife. That is all well and good of course, but what of the people who have seen ghostly images of people running at them with a hatchet or carrying around a lantern, dressed to the nines in vintage clothing and the latest Victorian footwear? Well, that leads us into the second classification.

Haunting: This is the one that really confuses people. The term is used not just for this classification, but also for a place that is beset with activity. As a result, when you mention a haunting, people just think you are talking about a place with activity as opposed to a particular type of activity. It's frustrating and confusing, but it is what it is. If you throw the term "residual" in front of it, you can avoid some of this confusion. What it is, as it turns out, is not really a ghost. At least it's not a ghost in the same way that an apparition is. Oddly, it's what most people think of when they think of a ghost. Essentially, a haunting phenomenon is when you see the image of a person or thing, complete with clothing and accessories, doing some repetitive behavior in a particular place. So if you have a troop movement of Civil War soldiers cutting through your kitchen at 8 p.m. every Wednesday...*that* would be a residual haunting.

How does this differ from an apparition aside from the clothing and objects? The most fundamental way is that there is nothing else *to* a haunting. There is no intelligence, awareness, or substance to the haunting. It's believed to be a recording of some emotionally-charged event that occurred at that place at that moment. So if you see someone running around with a chainsaw swinging it like he's killing people, then it's probably the recording of some sort of traumatic chainsaw massacre. That, or it's an amateur theater production gone terribly awry. In either case, it's certainly best to act with prudence.

Sometimes people have a hard time wrapping their brains around this idea, as if somehow a recording on space and time is any more ridiculous in concept than disembodied spirits wandering around. In reality, it's much less far-fetched. The molecules that make up our bodies change every seven years, meaning that every seven years we are made up of entirely different parts. If the molecules that make up our bodies lacked the ability to pass information from one cell to another, then we would look, act, and sound different every seven years. As it is, however, we don't even notice the changeover and are pretty much the same people we have always been. When you apply this to the space around us, and everything around us is made of molecules, it isn't such a stretch to imagine that locations could record events the same way you might with a video camera. In the case of a haunting, the images recorded are essentially replayed over and over, usually at regular intervals. Typically, these events are emotionally-charged and often traumatic. For whatever reason, emotions tend to factor into this, although why that is the case remains unknown.

The litmus test for whether something is an apparition or a haunting is, "does it have clothes and objects and does it do the same things repetitively?" If the answer to those questions is yes, then you have a haunting going on. At the very least, you can rest assured that you are not dealing with something that can affect you in any way, and if planned correctly, can be great fun at dinner parties.

Poltergeist: This is the most popular of all the categories of ghosts, particularly for horror writers and filmmakers. It's easy to understand why as poltergeist activity is very dynamic and exciting, or, possibly, terrifying depending on who you are. Poltergeist means noisy spirit and refers to a type of activity in which objects are flung around the room; paintings and pictures drop off the walls; dressers and bookcases move or fall down; pretty much anything not nailed down, and even sometimes things that are, being manipulated around a room by an unseen force. The notion that something with sentience could start throwing things around like an unhinged, quarreling spouse is truly a terrifying proposition. Terrifying as it may be, it's also a bit of a misrepresentation.

As mentioned earlier, nothing is set in stone in the paranormal. Since it's all best guesses, there is no definitive rule at this point. Despite that, these classifications are the product of as scientific a study as could be managed and all the evidence points to their validity. What years upon years of research says about poltergeists is simply that they are not ghosts at all, but rather the unconscious, unleashed psychokinetic energy generating from some human source within the location. To clarify, **psychokinesis** *is a phenomenon that was once referred to as telekinesis and is the ability to manipulate objects with a person's mind*. The term telekinesis hasn't been used in the paranormal community for quite some time, but society at large never got the memo, so there is often confusion between the two terms, and quite often the general public won't know what it is outside of something a serial killer might use.

In the case of the poltergeist, the person responsible for the activity is completely unaware of it and is often an adolescent going through puberty and all the emotional confusion and discord that comes along with it. Again, this is not absolute. The source person, or agent, could be any age and of any sex. The one constant here is that there is almost always some emotional disturbance present for this activity to occur. Usually shiny, happy people don't make things fly across the room with their minds...at least not unintentionally.

This is usually when someone raises his hand and says that he knows a story where there are real ghosts and there's poltergeist activity and did you learn ghost busting out of a Cracker Jack box? The answers, in no particular order are, no, I prefer Crunch and Munch, I do not bust any ghosts, and poltergeist activity and other types of activity are not mutually exclusive. Not only can you have two types, but you can also have all three—and it's more common than one might think. What tends to happen when you see these occurring at the same time is that the apparition or haunting is scaring someone, which stresses them out and causes them to lash out with their mind. That, added to the other paranormal activity, scares them even more and feeds into itself until you have an unending cycle that would be more suitable as a movie of the week on *Lifetime*.

The above is not to say that it's impossible for an apparition to be able to manipulate objects. The general scientific consensus is that they cannot; however, in our experience with paranormal activity I have found more than one incident in which objects were manipulated when no one else was around and, therefore, could not credibly be responsible for the moved objects. In these cases, however, people will find objects missing or will come home to find them moved around as opposed to things being thrown or dancing in mid air in front of them. The nature of the activity is important to distinguish that which might be an actual apparition versus a poltergeist activity.

Are There Symptoms of a Haunted House?

You may be wondering, "Exactly how do people determine if their home or business is haunted?" Barring a full-scale investigation with lots of highly scientific equipment and flashy night-vision cameras to capture all manner of full-bodied apparitions, there are a few more subtle examples of how regular old paranormal activity behaves:

Noises – This is easily one of the most common occurrences when it comes to a haunted house. People often describe hearing sounds like creaking floorboards, footsteps, or even the sound of someone calling their name. Most often, this presents as faint whispers and suggestions that can easily be dismissed. This type of activity is so insidious that people often automatically assume they are "just hearing things" or that it's "just their imagination." By the time the phantom noises advance to full-scale piano concertos, the occupants have already considered a padded cell at Shady Acres and one of those jackets with really long sleeves and all the fancy buckles in the back.

Shadows – Not only are people hearing things, but they are also seeing things. Rarely does an apparition or evidence of a haunting appear directly and brazenly in front of a witness (although it's certainly not unheard of). More often, apparitions are seen as fleeting movement in one's peripheral vision, making assertions of paranormal activity much more easily dismissed as sleep deprivation or tired eyes. Perhaps this is just nature's way of acclimating people to the impending barrage of extrasensory overload, but most activity, including apparitions, start small and increase gradually over time.

Disappearing Stuff – This may be the most maddening by-product of paranormal activity out of all of them. What starts out as "have you seen my sunglasses?" quickly becomes a full-scale teardown of the entire house, searching everything from counters to dresser drawers to attic crawlspaces, only to have the offending item reappear days or weeks later, in exactly the spot where you thought you left it in the first place and subsequently checked fifty times. Seriously, this will drive a man to drink — if he could just remember where he left the vodka.

This is really just the broadest possible description of potential paranormal activity. By no means does the presence of any or all of these experiences prove positively that a given place is haunted. These are just a few common threads that people routinely describe when discussing their own situations. It is just as possible that anyone with these complaints is sleepy, forgetful, or just plain stressed out. This is merely to illustrate just how normal and unspectacular a haunting or apparition can be, and therefore how completely normal it is...well, that's what we think, anyway.

Why Tucson?

I guess the real question here is: Why NOT Tucson? Tucson has been inhabited as far back as 10,000 BCE by our Neanderthal ancestors, and has been gaining in population ever since. Based on that timeframe, you are looking at over 12,000 years of natural death, murder, suicide, massacre, and general unpleasantness. Now, obviously everyone is going to die at one point, giving the human race a one hundred percent mortality rate, but since entering the modern age, the causes of death have become more varied and spectacular. People aren't just withering and dying in their beds, surrounded by loved ones anymore. They're being shot at while pumping gas, hacked to death and buried in the foundation of a small strip mall business, run over by irresponsible drunks who will never know when to say "when," or even assaulted while they sleep in some manner of home-invasion. It's absolutely sickening the abject lack of care that people seem to have developed towards each other — although, if you ASKED anyone, they would vehemently deny being a part of the social indifference that begets such unspeakable acts. Nevertheless, people die violently here on a daily basis. I don't know how that compares to the rest of the nation, but for our purposes, it certainly validates the point that we are trying to make: Tucson's got ghosts.

We have already mentioned a few of Tucson's more well-known haunts in *Scare-Izona: A Travel Guide To Arizona's Spookiest Spots* — the ghost girl of Colossal Cave Mountain Park, the numerous ghosts that haunt the Hotel Congress, or the elusive but prankish ghost of the Fox Theatre — but what we will embrace in this book are not the paranormal investigations that we have experienced, but the stories told to us by friends, family, and complete strangers — those who comprise the front lines of paranormal activity. They deal with it every day whether at home or at work or...sometimes they are lucky enough to experience activity in both places. These are the people this book is about. Some see it from "the glass is half-full" perspective and some see the glass as "half-empty." Still, others see the glass float across their kitchen while they cower in the cabinets beneath the sink.

Aside from a few notable exceptions, the stories come directly from the people who experienced them. We have not investigated these locations because A) access and time (on the part of the property owners) both tend to come in very limited quantities when the words "ghost hunt" or "paranormal investigation" get bandied about, and B) this book celebrates the experiences of regular people who do not claim any affiliation to the paranormal whatsoever. These are just ordinary folks who, during the course of a normally uneventful day, experienced something they cannot explain in definitive terms.

As for the locations, these are just normal homes or businesses that happen to have a reputation for being haunted. Sometimes the activity is only experienced by one person during an isolated incident, and sometimes it is so common that it's considered part of the daily routine. In any case, these stories, particularly those involving local businesses, should not be a deterrent from patronizing these establishments. We believe that having a ghost around can only enhance the visit, and we also lovingly embrace the idea that part of Tucson's history remains alive – if in *spirit* – to remind us of our roots. As always, be respectful when visiting any of the public locations.

Between the three of us, we have spent several decades living in this city and that, along with our investigative credentials, puts us in the advantageous position of being able to share these stories with everyone who wants to take a peek into the lives of these folks who, by now, have just grown to accept that they are truly never alone. We are the members of Wailing Bansidhe Investigations and we reside in Tucson. Although we have investigated all over the great state of Arizona, we hold our Tucson ghosts very near and dear to our hearts because they live — or, rather, DON'T live — in our own backyard.

Since the focus of the book is to make people more comfortable with their own ghosts, as well as the entire topic of the paranormal, we thought we might kick off the storytelling with our own personal experiences living right here in the Old Pueblo.

1
Who Are We?

We would like to take some time and introduce ourselves and to reinforce why it is we know what we are talking about. We are collectively the members of Wailing Bansidhe Investigations, an organization dedicated to investigating the paranormal, and, as such, we have investigated dozens of haunted places in Arizona, documenting a great deal of them in our previous book, *Scare-Izona: A Travel Guide to Arizona's Spookiest Spots.*

J. Patrick Ohlde is a graduate of the University of Arizona, holding a bachelor's degree in psychology. While at the University of Arizona, he took William Everist's parapsychology class and went on to join Pima Community College's paranormal investigation group. After several investigations with that group, he joined Katie and Mikal in forming Wailing Bansidhe Investigations.

Katie Mullaly has a lengthy history of her own unexplainable personal experiences, leading to an all-consuming interest in the field of the paranormal. After learning formal technique as a student of William Everist, she joined forces with husband, Mikal, and J. Patrick Ohlde to create Wailing Bansidhe Investigations. In addition to co-writing *Scare-Izona: A Travel Guide to Arizona's Spookiest Spots*, Katie has been a contributing writer of haunted locations for several local publications.

Mikal Mullaly has had an experience or two of his own, but still prefers to be the resident "voice of reason." He is the webmaster, tech guy, driver, event coordinator, stylist, and nutritionist of the group. He has also been tested with a high level of telepathic ability, and has his own built-in ghost of some sort that has been following him since he was nineteen years old. In typical debunking fashion, he prefers not to let that cloud his reasoning, and always tries to find logic in the illogical. Barring that, he enjoys rolling his eyes and throwing his arms up in exasperation.

In addition to these academic achievements and formal experiences in paranormal investigation, both Katie and Patrick found themselves growing up in haunted houses. Not only did these childhood experiences become the catalyst for their friendship and writing endeavors, including on paranormal websites of their creation, but it also formed the foundation for this book. Besides having had professional experience investigating the paranormal, they have experience being unwitting participants in activity they could not understand. They know what it's like to be afraid, unsure, and feel crazy. They were once right where you are.

Patrick's Ghostly Experiences

One potential lesson a person can learn from my experiences growing up is this: If you have small children and live in a haunted house, your first inclination to not tell them about the activity to keep them from being scared may not be the correct one. I moved into my childhood home in Tucson when I was three, after having to essentially flee Oregon as I had life-threatening asthma and had pneumonia nine times. Nothing was mentioned to my parents regarding the activity when they purchased the house, an oversight they sought to use as a way to terminate the sale within the first week of living there, but they were locked into the deal and the house would be theirs for some twenty-five years.

The activity began right away, although it was unspecific and more off-putting than anything downright terrifying. As with many disturbances, it was characterized by creepy feelings and the sense that you were just not alone. Generally, these feelings were more prevalent at night, although they were not exclusive to just the nighttime hours. Given these strange feelings, my parents started to look into the history of the place and found, in relatively short order, that one of the house's previous owners had been killed in the driveway. According to the neighbors, the man had been working on his car and the jacks fell out from under the car and he was crushed. That original family moved out and another moved in, but they didn't stay terribly long, and then we came along. I would imagine the shortness of tenure for the previous family led to our not being told of the death, but it's a detail that requires disclosure when selling a house. As it was, my parents were not told, but they still couldn't back out.

It would be easy enough to write off the creepy feelings as less than legitimate, especially in light of the new information regarding the death in the driveway. One could assume that the new information just added fuel to an already crackling fire and that from then on out even the most ambiguous strange occurrence would be attributed to the man who had died. That would have been a safe assumption had the disturbances not graduated from the general to the very specific. Everything changed one night... the general and vague feelings of uneasiness turned into very specific feelings of fear.

My dad was working graveyard at the time and my mom stayed up late reading as a matter of habit. Sometime in the late hours of the night or early hours of the morning, depending on how one looked at it, a figure appeared next to her and seemed to be reading over her shoulder. Obviously, this was fairly startling as figures, typically, don't materialize out of nowhere in one's peripheral vision and proceed to leer behind you. My mom turned to see what it was and the figure, little more than a black silhouette, promptly disappeared. At that moment she was completely done with the house and wanted to move.

Moving was not an option and at the time my fairly logical-minded dad found himself dubious of the occurrence. Time would change his mind as this sort of thing began to happen on a fairly regular basis. Another such incident — one that made my dad start to come around and is to this day one of his favorite stories to tell — involved a friend of the family visiting and having a fitful night in which he would get very little sleep. He was sleeping on the floor in the living room and shortly after going to sleep he awoke to see someone scurrying down the hallway. He thought it must have been me and attempted to drift back off to sleep. This lasted only a few moments as, again, he was awakened to find someone moving quickly down the hall. At this point, he decided it was time to alert my parents that I was awake and up to some manner of shenanigans. A quick, bleary-eyed inspection found me fast asleep and a fair amount shorter than the figure our friend had seen. Still, it was mostly the movement he was tracking rather than any clear vision of the figure in question, so it was an honest enough mistake. He tried to go back to sleep. Several minutes later, he was back up and telling my parents that he KNEW I had to be awake because he had seen someone in the hall a third time. Again, I was found to be fast asleep. The rest of the night progressed just like this with our friend seeing a figure in the hall, little more than a shadow moving around. My parents offered the theory that it was the ghost, but our friend did not believe in such things and refused to accept it at first. Eventually, however, after several sightings that night, he came around to believe that there was something more than natural going on in the house.

It wasn't just sightings of the figure, either; objects were sometimes manipulated in various forms. My dad tells a story—the one that turned him from philistine to believer—of cleaning a coffee maker and disassembling it to better clean each piece. My parents laid out each of the pieces in a particular order so none would be lost, taking particular notice of each piece's location. When the time came for reassembly, they found a piece missing. My parents looked everywhere for the missing piece and after over an hour of searching they came up empty. Finally, my dad suggested they leave for a while and come back, convinced that the "ghost" had taken the piece. So they did just that. They left and came back two hours later only to find the piece precisely where they had originally left it and had subsequently checked several times.

Another instance came after we returned from a family vacation. Prior to our return, my grandmother and aunt came over to turn on the swamp cooler and clean the house so it would be cool and in order when we returned. How it would have been any more or less messy than when we left is something of a mystery to me, but it was a courtesy my aunt and grandma wanted to provide. When they left some two hours before our return, they swear everything was in order and put away; however, when we arrived at the house we found every door, window, cabinet, and drawer wide open. The chairs were also all sitting on top of the kitchen table. My parents immediately suspected burglary and were very alarmed. I was alarmed as well—as my most prized possession, a Hippity Hop, was in the house and I reasoned that such an item must be fixed solidly at the top of any burglar's hit list. My parents found said Hippity Hop for me and got me fixated on that while they made a quick circuit of the house to inventory their possessions. As it turns out, nothing was missing at all. Jewelry, electronics, money; none of it was touched. My parents immediately suspected another culprit. Sure, it's been bandied around that my aunt and grandma were playing some sort of trick, but the amount of time and effort it would take to open all things able to be opened in the house and then never, in over twenty years, take credit for it makes this an unlikely scenario. Pursuant to their policy of nondisclosure, I remained blissfully unaware that their final suspect was, in fact, an apparition.

Obviously, from the first week we lived in the house, a decision was made not to tell me about any of this business for fear that I would be terrified and paranoid. In their opinion, I was better served in this by ignorance. However, my parents did not take into consideration the possibility that I would see this figure on my own and debate very seriously, over the course of about six years, whether or not I was completely insane.

The first time I remember seeing anything myself was probably when I was around seven or eight. I was up late reading; I read every night when I went to bed, and the way that my bed was situated in the room, I could see into the hallway. My parents' bedroom was directly across the hallway and I could see if someone were, say, walking into my parents' room. This is precisely what happened—and it happened often. The first time it happened, I doubted what I had seen. I *knew* I saw someone go in there, but I didn't know who it was. I saw the figure as nothing more than a silhouette and didn't recognize it as one of my parents. Obviously curious, and not aware of anything I should be scared of, I ventured out to see who it was. I crossed the hallway and found my parents' room dark and empty. I crept back down the hallway, careful not to let them know I was up and out of bed, and saw that they were watching TV in the den.

I decided that I had just imagined it, and settled back into my reading, but I didn't feel nearly as safe and comfortable as I had before. In subsequent nights, over the course of the next six or seven years, I saw the figure at least three or four times a week. I gave up on trying to catch whoever it was and I resigned myself to the notion that I was, in fact, crazy. I never even asked my parents about it out of fear of being exposed as a crazy person. When my grandpa gave me a record (that's right, an actual vinyl record) of the Legend of Sleepy Hollow, the full impact of my street's name, Sleepy Hollow, collapsed upon me like a cave-in and I not only feared a ghost in the house, but also became convinced that the headless horseman was stalking the street and would invariably be hiding in the gap between the bed and the wall. I slept with the covers drawn up to my neck every night, a practice I still must do to be able to sleep, more out of habit than an overriding fear of Washington Irving's creation, and kept the door open and lights on. My belief as a child was that I was safer this way, but looking back it occurs to me that if there were monsters and madmen lurking the halls, I was essentially providing them with unobstructed passage and plenty of light to set upon me by. As it was, I was just making it easier to see the man in the hallway going into my parents' room. It's common for children to be afraid of the dark and of monsters, but it makes it so much worse when there *really is* something lurking there in the dark of the hallway.

I don't remember what age I was when I finally found out, by way of my cousin, that the place was haunted. I remember being upset and relieved all at the same time. I was annoyed to not have been told and relieved that I was not crazy, at least not any crazier than my parents, anyway. Of course, in retrospect, I understand their desire to protect me from things that were obviously scary. You throw in my abject fear of Freddy Krueger and it seems a forgone conclusion that I should not be told. Still, I think an argument could be made that I was more susceptible to the fear of such things simply because I was convinced I was crazy and saw on a regular basis someone I couldn't explain.

Eventually, my bed was moved, so I didn't see the ghost going into my parents' room anymore...but that wasn't the end to my sightings and experiences. Again, these experiences fell into a wide range of activity. The most common experience involved the apparition standing in my doorway watching whatever I was doing, whether it was playing video games or watching TV. This became much more of a nuisance and an annoyance than anything scary or creepy. Particularly once I entered my teen years, the lack of privacy became very bothersome. For whatever reason, it would never enter my room, just stand at the doorway watching. I would see the shadow out of the corner of my eye and generally if I told it aloud to go away it would do so. I tried, for a time, to just close the door, but time and time again the door would open and I would feel someone staring into the room at me. I am willing to concede that my mom could have been checking on me, but the timing of the door opening to when I closed it tended to suggest that she wasn't the one doing it.

More specific and scarier experiences also happened from time to time. The first major event occurred during my sophomore year in high school. I was home alone and on the phone with a friend while playing a computer game in the entertainment room just off the TV room. The room shared a wall with the garage, and I was sitting very close to the door that opened into our TV room. As I sat prattling on about the sort of things that teenage geeks playing games on the computer might be talking about,

31

I saw someone rush towards me from the TV room. The figure advanced with enormous speed. I turned to see who it was and *it* disappeared just inches from my face as I completed my head turn. I screamed like a little girl, much to the amusement of my friend who had been in the middle of some sort of diatribe regarding chess openings. In all the times I've seen the ghost, this incident was the most startling. I was there alone and seeing someone run at me did not initially trigger thoughts of the ghost, but rather some crazy person who had broken into my house. Having said person then disappear did little for my heart rate, and indeed whatever reputation I held amongst my friends as far as bravery was concerned. (Still, I defy said friend to have a shadow run up on him at full speed only to disappear inches from his face and not scream at the top of his lungs and/or wet himself.)

Another startling encounter, which also involved the phone, occurred a year later. It was around midnight and I was talking to my girlfriend at the time and sort of pacing around the house, as I was wont to do. I was in the kitchen and I heard keys rattling in the front door. My cousin, who was living with us at the time, was coming home, and I moved toward the doorway leading into the living room and the hallway. As I got to the point where I could see the front door, a man ran into the hall from the living room right in my field of vision. My first reaction was that it was my cousin, but at that moment the front door swung open and my cousin came in. I just stood there staring, with my girlfriend talking in my ear, and my cousin asked, "What? Did you see the ghost?" and I asked him if he saw it, to which he replied, "No, but you are completely white and look like you've seen a ghost." I stepped into the living room and looked down the hall, which was dark and empty.

The hallway is something of a hot spot for activity for some reason. The ghost has been seen in other parts of the house, but the hallway seems to dominate the sightings. By extension, the hall bathroom has seen action from time to time as well. Often, the bathroom would just have bouts of the chills, where you get some unmotivated shiver in the room, but at least on one occasion, I walked by the bathroom door in broad daylight and caught a figure standing in the bathroom at the sink. I thought it was my grandma, who was in the house with me at the time, but I turned the corner into the kitchen to find her standing at that sink. I backed up and looked back in the bathroom and found it empty.

The most horrifying of my encounters in the house — and the only one that really "scared" me in any meaningful way — occurred again in high school. Once again, it was around midnight and I was ending a phone conversation and went to the bathroom before bed. The hallway was dark as I didn't bother turning on the light and, as I got to the bathroom, I heard the sounds of talking and laughing coming from the TV room. At first blush I thought it was some kind of talk show, with a host telling the monologue and the audience laughing. I didn't think much of it as I reasoned it must just be my cousin up watching TV. As I was coming out of the bathroom, I noticed two disturbing things. First, the sound, which had disappeared when I was in the bathroom despite having a window that opened into the TV room, was back as I stood in the hallway. The second was that I could hear my cousin snoring in his bedroom right across the hall. I opened the door and peeked in and there he was sleeping. I went through the kitchen and into the TV room to see if the TV was still on. Not only did the sound stop as I entered the kitchen, but the TV didn't even have that glow it has when it's just been turned off. It was pitch black and had obviously not been on for quite some time. I turned and went back into the hallway, and as I reached the bathroom I heard the sounds again, this time not coming from the TV room but rather from the living room, just a few feet away from me. I moved down the hallway toward my bedroom and the sound followed, the previously indistinguishable voices starting to sound an awful lot like "he's alone" followed by laughter. I reached my bedroom, turned off the light, shut the door, and dove in bed all in one fluid movement that by all rights should have resulted in, at the very least, a broken jaw and missing teeth. I managed to sleep after a couple of hours and I never heard any of the sounds again.

I lived in this house until I was 23, so I experienced MANY things over the years. Most were much more mundane and routine than the above stories and sort of served to desensitize me to the "scary" part of the paranormal experience. I might still side with the "crazy" prognosis I gave myself earlier in life, though, if it weren't for the sightings by other people unrelated to the family that occurred on a fairly regular basis over the years. The typical requirement for an experience in my house was that the person in question had to be spending the night. Daytime sightings, while not unheard of, were fairly rare.

One of the most notable of these sightings — and this is one of my favorites if only because it changed the mind of a skeptic — happened again in high school when a friend of mine was spending the night. My friend didn't believe in ghosts. We had the most bitter of debates about it for years and I was completely incensed by the notion that he believed in psychokinesis, but not the possibility of ghosts. The idea that it was possible that you could move an object with your mind but that ghosts were silly made my head want to explode. At any rate, his mind was changed, which put the argument to bed once and for all. On the night in question, we were sleeping in my cousin's room since there were two beds in that room. The bed in which I was sleeping was against the wall and his was closer to the door. I slept just fine, but when I woke up the next morning and looked at my friend, he was wide-eyed and staring at the ceiling. Puzzled, I asked him what was wrong. He told me that he thought he had seen the ghost. I thought he was kidding at first and tossed him the sort of dismissive expletive that you would when you think you are being mocked, but the conviction, and indeed fear, on his face told me such a dismissal was unwarranted. Apparently, around three in the morning he had woken to find a figure, nothing more than a black silhouette, enter the room through the closed door, walk around his bed to the foot of my bed, and stand in front of the window. It appeared to be looking out the window and then slowly turned its head and "looked" at me and then eventually vanished. My friend didn't sleep the rest of the night and has been a believer in ghosts ever since.

My friends experienced several other sightings, from seeing someone walking down the hallway to seeing a figure standing in the living room. Time and time again the reports were consistent with past activity and often the people reporting the activity were unaware there was a ghost at all. When you live in a haunted house, you don't talk about it that much just out of fear of being called crazy at best or a liar at worst. So it wasn't particularly advertised, and yet people kept seeing things over and over.

Katie's Ghostly Experiences

It would be impossible not to have an interest in the paranormal after having lived in as many active places as I have thus far in my lifetime. My first indication that our family did not reside alone in our home came when I was a teenager. Shortly after we moved into that home, my grandmother passed away in one of the bedrooms. My sister and I had been sharing a room, but after my grandmother's death, my sister took up residency in her room. On her first night in the room after my grandmother's passing, my sister awoke to find that a small chair, handcrafted by my previously deceased grandfather, had been placed next to her bed from its normal spot across the room, and the crucifix had been removed from the wall and placed on the chair. Not really comprehending the oddity of the situation, my sister simply placed the cross back on the wall and moved the chair back into the corner from whence it came. Of course, once she actually relayed the details of this incident and discovered that it was not done by any living hands in the house, we all shuddered at exactly how creepy it was.

Although that bedroom was always the most intimidating room in the house — it was never anything but cold and sterile — it was by no means the only part of the house that saw activity. I can specifically recall many evenings being left alone while the rest of my family was out. I would hear knocking noises and voices and the feeling of the house was incredibly heavy and frightening. On one such occasion, I let my dog into the house to keep me company only to be even more disturbed by the fact that she sat in front of an empty armchair, gazing intently at an unseen occupant, actually going as far as putting her paw into the chair in an apparent attempt to coax affection. From that point on, my dog and I spent the rest of our evening sitting in the driveway of the house, waiting for my parents to come home.

As anyone can imagine, living under these circumstances as a perpetually frightened teenage girl made it necessary to go to great lengths NOT to be caught alone in the dark. To this end, I was forced to schedule any middle-of-the-night trips to the bathroom to coincide with my brother's usual return time of 2 a.m. The inconvenient side effect of his preferred social activities was a very predictable late-night case of the munchies. I knew that it would be safe to use the bathroom when I heard his footsteps in the kitchen and the unmistakable sound of a utensil scraping the inside of a jar of Miracle Whip or applesauce. On one such occasion, I can recall hearing the sound of his meal preparation, and being particularly relieved to be able to dash to the restroom, only to find myself standing in a darkened hallway with absolutely no indication of the aforementioned activity. At that point, however, I was committed to my trip to the bathroom and could no longer wait for anyone to rescue me. Once inside the bathroom, I actually considered spending the rest of the night in there, safely ensconced in the comforting glow of four 100-watt light bulbs.

Since that first experience of living with a "ghost," I have had exceptional luck moving into houses and apartments that have the added bonus of paranormal activity. When my oldest son was a toddler, I lived in a perfectly respectable apartment in a relatively new apartment complex near the neighborhood of Broadway and Camino Seco. From the very first day that I lived there, I never felt comfortable being alone. It started with a vague sense of always being watched, and that quickly turned into a yearlong series

A strange anomaly appeared in this photo taken in Katie's apartment. It was not visible when the photo was taken.

of unexplainable annoyances, ranging from apparitions peering around corners and dashing across the room, to items moving of their own accord. I would like to say that the activity seemed to center around the dining room, but the apartment was so small that it probably doesn't even matter.

I think one of the most disturbing occurrences included my son, sitting in his crib, focused on an upper corner of the room and jabbering away just as though someone were standing there talking to him. The other incident that gave me pause was a bath towel that perpetually removed itself from the towel bar while I showered. I will clarify that I was alone at home with my toddler son, who was in his crib, and the bathroom door was securely closed. I placed the towel, which I took fresh from the dryer, evenly on the towel bar and got into the shower. When I got out, the towel was piled on the floor. The door never opened and there was no noise. Obviously the ghost had a good sense of humor because it happened on more than one occasion. I was never more relieved than the day I moved out of that apartment.

Another strange anomaly. It apparently moved with Katie into her current house.

I am now living in your basic, run-of-the-mill ranch-style house on the east side of Tucson — four bedrooms, two baths, and *one poltergeist*. Now, in all fairness, a poltergeist isn't a "thing" as much as it's an activity, but there is definitely some combination of energy that is responsible for doorknobs rattling, music boxes winding themselves and playing (without disturbing the thick coating of dust), and every cabinet door in the house being opened to greet me bright and early in the morning. Honestly, I blame Mikal. He moved in and brought his wacky, yet lovable, misaligned chakra into the home and high jinks ensued. I often wonder if anyone else on the block awakens in the middle of the night to the sound of a metal stepstool moving itself in the hallway, or pictures flying from the walls and crashing to the ground. Some people would be entirely too frightened to live in a house like this, but a girl's gotta have something to write about, doesn't she?

††††††††††††††††

In a recent conversation with a colleague regarding ghosts (imagine that!), I suddenly recalled an experience I had at a previous job some time ago. This particular job was processing medical claims for a local hospital network, which amounted to opening mail and removing staples, in a building located in the vicinity of Grant Avenue and I-10. Now, it's important to note that, for the most part, I loathed the job and the people with whom I worked (with a few notable exceptions) because they were all incredibly catty and nasty to me. When they offered me (after several rounds of shameless begging) the opportunity to work second shift hours, I jumped at the chance. I was just back from maternity leave, and now could do my job without the distraction of the seething hatred that filled me much in the same way that Boston Crème fills a doughnut.

Of course, any place you go tends to have its own set of rumors circulating about parts of a building being haunted, or someone having committed suicide, or a construction worker who died while the building was being built, or perhaps even that the building was built over a burial ground (unless, of course, you happen to be writing a book about it, then the stories dry up like the floor of the Bonneville Salt Flats, but I digress). It is very difficult to substantiate any such stories because they are frequently exaggerations at best and completely untrue at worst. This particular building was no different, and the stories of the second floor being haunted would pop up occasionally, although I was never clear on the exact circumstances of the haunting.

I began working nights and my work life improved significantly. I befriended the security guard, Justin, and spent half my time socializing and half my time working. The one downside to working alone at night in an area that usually houses about seventy-five people is the sensation that you are being watched. You are not tucked away in your own little office, and you feel like you are on display for some unseen audience. This place was no different, so I just chalked it up to being all by myself on a dark and quiet floor. One evening in particular, I was sitting at my desk, waiting for Justin to show up so we could walk to the convenience store on the corner, when I heard footsteps coming down the tile walkway towards the section where I was sitting. I remember thinking that it didn't quite sound like his footsteps because they were lighter and did not match the "step, jingle" pattern caused by the keys hanging on one side of his belt.

As the steps got closer, I grabbed some cash out of my purse. I waited for a few more seconds, expecting him to round the corner, but he didn't. I got up from my desk and started towards the walkway, expecting to see him standing in one of the carpeted aisles. When I got to the walkway, I had a clear view of the entire floor. There was no Justin. I stood for just a second, feeling even more exposed than I had been, when out of the corner of my eye I saw movement. It was several rows away, but it looked like someone had seen me and ducked down out of my sight. I tentatively walked towards the area where I had seen the image, and in doing so I walked past a heavy wooden door that led to the stairwell. As I stepped past the door, I heard three loud knocks on the door. Startled, but undaunted, I peered through the small square window to see if anyone was there (which would have been scary in a whole different way) but, as I suspected, no one was in the stairway. With my adrenaline pulsating every nerve and fiber in my body, I kept walking towards the row in which I had seen the figure moving. I slowly walked past every row, peeking down each one with the expectation that I might get pummeled by someone (or something) who was as surprised to see me as I was to see them.

By the time I reached the last row, I was now certain that there was no other person on the second floor with me. I immediately quickened my step and went downstairs looking for Justin. When I eventually caught up with him, I told him of my scary experience and he didn't seem terribly surprised by what I had to say. He then told me that at least one other person had an experience when she was leaving late one night. As she drove past the building, she looked up at the then-unoccupied second floor and felt the hair rise on the back of her neck when she saw a dark, shadowy figure looking back at her from the upstairs window — in the same area where I had seen it.

That was the only experience I had in that building, I suspect, partly, because I didn't work there for that much longer and because, with a group of newly hired temps, I never had to be alone on that floor again. A few months after this experience, the entire department was laid off, and I do not know who currently occupies that space. I have not been back to that building, but I would be very curious to know if the latest occupants have any reports of the dark, shadowy visitor.

By definition, this would fall under the category of an apparition. It lacked any manner of distinguishing features and appeared only as a shadow in both incidents. Furthermore, the fact that it ducked out of my line of sight when I spied it out of the corner of my eye suggests that it was aware of my presence and didn't want to be noticed more than it already had. Secondary to that, the knocking on the door would suggest that the energy seems to be serving as a catalyst for poltergeist activity. Although two different types of activity, they are not mutually exclusive and the energy required for both types of activity can actually perpetuate each other. If one is prone to creating poltergeist activity, the energy and intensity of an apparition (or haunting) can make that ability stronger.

One of the major challenges made by skeptics against the paranormal in general and ghosts in particular is the fact that documenting the phenomena is difficult if not outright impossible. The requirement of all scientific principles is the ability to recreate the effects in a lab. You simply cannot do that with a ghost or haunting phenomena. Many people take that to mean that it's a figment of an overactive imagination and is something that is completely ridiculous to talk about in a serious way. Most such people claim that they believe only what they can see, hear, and touch. We are those sorts of people as well, the difference being that we have done that our whole lives. We have seen, heard, and "touched" not just in our own homes, but also in other locations and situations. There are many experiences we have had which we will concede were caused by some normal thing and not anything supernatural, and we will always look for other explanations before declaring something as legitimate paranormal activity. On the same token, however, there are many things we cannot explain any other way. Skeptics often use **Occam's razor,** *the principle that says that the simplest explanation is most often the correct one*, to debunk the paranormal, but we have found many instances where the same principle can be applied to the conclusion that it is paranormal. Still, as with our previous book, we are not attempting to prove or disprove anything here. We are looking at ghost stories and experiences people have had in Tucson, Arizona, and offering our takes on what these experiences are. Some of the stories may be explained in less paranormal terms, but some of them cannot. In general, however, we are just looking to let people know that no, they are not crazy and no, they are not alone. If you have a problem with that, you may be more comfortable reading something by James Randi or Penn and Teller. If not, then let's dig into the stories... you'll know which one of us is narrating as our names will appear before our section(s).

2

Tucson's Most Haunted

The Dearly Departed

One Last Goodbye

Patrick

One of the unfortunate aspects of the paranormal as it applies to ghosts and haunting phenomena is that in order for there to be activity, someone has had to die. Usually people experience hauntings and ghostly encounters as a sort of impersonal event, the bumping into of two strangers, one of whom is no longer living. Those sorts of events are scary at worst and unsettling at best, but the whole experience takes on a whole new dimension when the "ghost" in question is not a stranger but rather a departed loved one. These events are often lighter on the scare factor and much heavier on the emotional side. Emotions can range from sadness and despair to happiness and a sense that everything is okay. This next story shows that sometimes, you get a bit of both thrown in for good measure.

††††††††††††††

When she was ten years old, Desiree lost her uncle in a car accident. It was obviously a tremulous time emotionally, especially for a little girl. Shortly after the accident, the girl and her mother moved into her uncle's house at Irvington and Kolb Roads, which was owned by her grandparents. A little less than a month went by and they tried to settle into the house amidst the loss and emotional turmoil at the time. Perhaps it was the heavy emotion and unrest that prompted what happened next.

Desiree was trying to sleep in her room and woke to find herself thirsty. After attempts were made to go back to sleep, she decided she would need to make a trip to the kitchen for a glass of water. She climbed out of bed and opened her bedroom door. When she stepped into the hall, the door to her mother's room, which was diagonal to her own room, opened and her mother also entered the hallway. She had also awakened due to thirst and was also on a trip to the kitchen for some water.

Mother and daughter began walking down the hallway toward the kitchen for their water, when there was a flash of light at the end of the hall and they saw a figure standing there. It was the girl's uncle. He stood there a moment, not a shadow or silhouette but a fully detailed version of the man, looking at them. The figure then waved and promptly disappeared.

For their part, the mother-and-daughter kitchen expeditionary team jumped back at the sight of uncle and brother popping into existence just feet from them and waving. When he was gone, Desiree asked her mother if she too had seen her uncle standing there waving, and her mother said that yes, in fact, she had. After a moment, they rejoined their mission for water and went back to bed, each feeling both creeped out and also a bit comforted. It was as if their beloved uncle and brother had come back to say goodbye and in doing so, reassure them that he was okay on some level. The event never repeated itself and the rest of their time spent in the house was uncolored by any further visitations. It was just that one, brief moment and then the quiet of normal.

In the years since, the two haven't really spoken of the incident, afraid, as so many are, that they will be considered "crazy." This is not one of the three most commonly reported experiences in haunted houses. The figure wasn't a shadow like an apparition, but didn't seem to follow any sort of pre-recorded activity like a haunting. Nothing was moved or manipulated. So how is this classified? What sort of phenomena is this? Are they crazy like they feared? As it turns out, it would appear that they had an experience shared by many others after a relative has died.

Investigator's comments

Looking at this story, it's almost the prototypical example of a crisis apparition. A **crisis apparition** *is a widely reported phenomenon that occurs when a person dies and appears to his or her loved ones and friends*. Typically, the apparition makes a gesture at the person it appears to, such as a wave or a nod or smile, just something to let them know it's okay. The apparition then disappears. Usually, the loved one has no idea there is anything wrong at all and calls to check on the person they just saw, only to find he or she has died suddenly.

Distance has no apparent bearing of any kind on this sort of occurrence as oftentimes the apparition appears to a loved one across the country or around the world. This phenomenon also seems to only occur in unexpected deaths. Typically, if someone is wasting away or expecting to die, loved ones are present anyway so it doesn't carry the same immediacy. In actuality, death doesn't even need to occur to prompt a crisis apparition. There have been reports, one of which even took place in Arizona, of people in peril appearing to friends and family to alert them of their danger. The Arizona incident is a good example of this as it involved a hiker in a canyon who broke his leg and was essentially stuck in the canyon, unable to move and wasting away in the heat. His image appeared to several loved ones who promptly sent out a search party and the man was rescued.

In the case of our story, however, one aspect of the experience is different than most other reported cases: the time. Typically, the apparition appears just moments after death occurs. Even an experience occurring hours after a death stretches the time frame a bit. So what would cause the lapse in time here? This is not an easy answer and illustrates that none of the rules of the paranormal are hard and fast. Certainly skeptics are likely to use this as justification for refuting the paranormal full stop, ignoring the fact that in this case two people witnessed the episode—and they both reported the same event. Life is rarely without exceptions and I doubt strongly that the paranormal would be any different.

As a matter of pure conjecture, it seems that the time gap between the event and the death could simply be in response to stress and welling-up emotion. Perhaps on some level, the uncle simply returned briefly to attempt to alleviate some of that stress. In a case like this, it's impossible to answer such a question as it's ultimately left up to a person's own sense of spirituality and beliefs and would be irresponsible to attempt to color that with our own feelings on the subject. Suffice it to say, this is most likely a crisis apparition with an irregular timeline. After all, we can't get planes to arrive on time, so how do we expect a ghost to manage?

‡‡‡‡‡‡‡‡‡‡‡‡

A Familiar Ghost

Katie

Since we have been writing this particular book about ghost stories, we have been receiving information from many directions. Friends, neighbors, co-workers, and sometimes even complete strangers have contributed to the text of this book, and all the stories are firsthand perspectives. One story that struck an interesting and particularly personal chord came to us from a recent acquaintance of my sister, and someone that – prior to hearing her tale – neither Patrick nor I had met.

Sarah told us of a family that lives in a suburb to the southeast of Tucson that were longtime friends of her own family for whom she would frequently babysit and housesit. Sadly, the mother of the family passed away very suddenly in a freak accident, the details of which are too specific to share without betraying the anonymity of the family. After the accident, Sarah said that items would start being moved mysteriously, only to turn up later in very odd places. On occasion, she would even have the physical sensation that someone was sitting on the edge of her bed in the guestroom when there was no one else in the room. This happened frequently enough that members of the family reported similar occurrences. Once an item went missing, it would not be found until the mother was acknowledged. When the husband of the deceased remarried, his new wife became a frequent target of the paranormal shenanigans. The frequency of the activity increased until one day, she finally had enough and sternly chastised the "ghost," firmly explaining that she was, in fact, dead and could no longer remain in the home. From that point on, the activity has lessened to a much more manageable level, occurring much less frequently, if at all.

What makes this tale even more bizarre is that, when I told Patrick the details of this story after having learned them from Sarah, he gave me a funny look and asked, "Was her last name Frobischer*?" I looked at my notes and confirmed that it was her last name. Then he looked like someone had let the air out of his soul. "Oh my God. Her husband was my friend. I went to her funeral."

(*Name has been changed.)

Investigator's comments:

It is truly a conundrum to find that someone you once knew could be causing paranormal activity that you are now studying. When someone close to you dies, you look for signs that he or she is still with you and waiting for you on the "other side," and this hope makes it possible to function in an otherwise despair-filled grief cycle. When there is just enough distance from the deceased to keep the heavy emotion from taking over, it gives an eerie sense of just how temporary and random our physical life is, cracking open a weird set of thoughts about the instantaneous and unexpected transition between alive and dead, and the spiritual and emotional perspective of the deceased.

From a paranormal perspective, the activity presents as textbook poltergeist. The stress of the sudden death of a family member could easily become a catalyst for misdirected grief. Once this happens, the affected individuals and their family members view the occurrences as signs from the deceased. When you introduce the variable of a new wife (who has now been told that paranormal activity is present and caused by the first wife, who was taken from the family suddenly and in her prime), you create more stress to fuel the untethered psychokinesis. Let me put it this way: try to imagine the terror that would consume you believing that your husband's dead first wife will haunt you for usurping her position...frankly, it's impressive that the entire house hasn't imploded at this point. Perhaps that is a bit of an exaggeration, but that level of emotional turmoil is very powerful, so it's no surprise that it could actually bleed over into a physical manifestation.

One Woman's Experiences

Patrick

Sometimes, though it's not as common as some of the other manifestations, activity can take the shape of other non-corporeal forms besides just mist or human-like figures. Flashes of light, smell, or sound can also be the chosen modality for the activity to take. In the next group of stories, we will see examples of this. These stories happened to the same person, Nicole Perdue, at distinctly different times in her life, and while one seems to be apropos of nothing, the others carry quite a bit more weight.

††††††††††††††

A Light in the Dark

The first story finds our friend, Nicole, in her bedroom late at night on the telephone. She was a freshman in high school at the time, so the late night phone conversation was a matter of course as it is for most teenagers. She was the only one awake and she was laying on her bed, which was facing her closed door. Aside from her whispered voice on the telephone, the place was as silent as it was dark.

Obviously, given the darkness in her room and in the hall, she did not expect a sudden surge of blue light to show under her door, but more alarming was when the light was suddenly blocked by something. It looked exactly as if someone were standing in front of the door for a moment and then, as quickly as it had come, the dark shape that blocked the light moved away. She could see the blue light again for a time before it too faded away.

She immediately asked her friend to hold on and got up and rushed into the hallway to see who was out there and what the source of light had been. In the hall she found nothing at all. The lights were all off and her mom was sound asleep in her bedroom. Nothing in the house was amiss or otherwise disrupted. Moving into the living room she checked the television to make sure it hadn't come on and gone off unexpectedly, but again, it was off and completely ordinary. Defeated, Nicole returned to her room and closed the door. She would never see anything like that again, although as you will know from one of her other stories in the book, this will not be the only time she came in contact with something strange out in the hallway.

✠✠✠✠✠✠✠✠✠✠✠✠

Conversation from Beyond

It should be apparent by now that paranormal activity takes all kinds of forms and will appear in a variety of different ways. For paranormal investigators, one of the most often overlooked but most significant manifestations are dreams. Most people disregard their dreams as a matter of course, not putting much stock in psychodynamics or other forms of dream interpretation; however, when investigating a haunted place during an overnight stay, dream journals are powerful tools.

Time and time again, it seems that spirits will use the dreams of the living to communicate or make their presence known. Some people reflexively scoff at this idea given that dreams are something of an altered state, but if you are allowing for ghosts in the first place, it's really not that big of a stretch to imagine that they can be felt in dreams. Add to that the successes in sensory replication researchers have had with dreams and you have something far too significant to discard out of hand.

Most often these dream encounters involve a personal connection with the spirit in question. This would mean it occurs exclusively in the dream state and usually the person doing the dreaming will present as the spirit or will see or communicate with the spirit. The dreams are usually vivid and seem exceptionally real. They also tend to be common to the place with people reporting the same sort of dreams time and time again.

Having said that, what happens when the experience extends out of the dream state and into something much more real? This next story will demonstrate that while we have many common occurrences, nothing is set in stone and as far as the paranormal is concerned, there is always something new in the dark.

It was late one summer night, somewhere between midnight and 1 a.m., when it happened. The now familiar Nicole, who was fifteen at the time, was reading a Stephen King novel on her bed, the recent loss of her father still fresh in her mind. It was one of those moments in life where, in the absence of outside verification, one would discard as the mind playing tricks. As it was, what would happen next became all too real.

Nicole's mother was sleeping in the next room and the house was totally quiet save for the sound of the turning of pages. It had been that way for quite some time that night so the sound of voices startled Nicole out of her reading. She sat frozen for several moments, hearing two distinct voices filtering through from her mother's room. That she and her mother were the only two in the house was only one of the startling elements here. The other was that the second voice was a man's voice in general and sounded like her father's voice in particular. Nicole's first thought was that her mother was talking in her sleep, but the fact that she had never done so before coupled with the notion that she would be doing a voice to fill in the second part of the conversation made Nicole think that something else might be going on.

Eventually the voices died down and Nicole could sleep, but the next day she had not forgotten what she had heard. With the sort of trepidation one approaches a situation that may make them look silly, Nicole asked her mother if she had had any weird dreams the night before. Her mom looked at her suspiciously and was quiet for a moment and asked why she was asking. Nicole just asked again, and again her mom asked why with a look of fear in her eyes. Seeing this could go on and on, Nicole told her mom that she had heard two distinct voices coming from her mom's room. Surprise tore across her mother's face, and after a moment she said that she had a dream in which Nicole's father had visited. In her dream, he came and sat on the edge of the bed and spoke with her at length before finally getting up and leaving.

This shocked both Nicole and her mother...as it was apparent that the dream had been something more than a dream. Nicole never heard the voices again and her mother never reported having more dreams featuring her father. Both had been ready to let the whole thing go as either hearing things or wishful dreaming, but in the end, they had to admit that it was real. A fanciful imagination can hardly account for two people experiencing the same thing at the same time, even if the modality of that experience was different for each. Regardless of the differences in actual experience, the event left them both with a sense of closure they had previously not been afforded.

Investigator's comments

This sort of incident is something of an anomaly. It has elements of a few different sorts of encounters, but doesn't necessarily exemplify any one in particular. There are the obvious *dream elements*, the *audio elements*, and the *crisis apparition element*. Usually in these sorts of cases, it would be said that several types of activity can exist alongside one another, but in this case, it would seem that it was all the same thing thrown together like an ethereal stew.

It seems like the simplest explanation would be that it was a visitation to make up for a loss of closure in the relationship. That is pretty much the method of operation for a crisis apparition, but this seemed a bit more prolonged and intimate than your garden-variety event of that type. Whatever romantic notions my cynicism hasn't killed off yet tend to explain it simply that Nicole's father came back to settle things and say goodbye. The how's and the why's of it are anyone's guess, really. This isn't the sort of thing that is easily explained away or categorized. Often those sorts of things are discarded, given that usually when something doesn't fit or sounds too outside the realms of past experience it is usually untrue. In this case, given that two people have had similar experiences independently of one another, it cannot just be summarily dismissed. So, it seems it must be chalked up to a variation on common occurrences and be left at that. It is quite a comforting story to think that you can have a chance for one more conversation with a lost loved one. Certainly it's not common, but being unique is not the same thing as being untrue. Maybe there is some romanticism left in the universe after all.

‡‡‡‡‡‡‡‡‡‡‡‡

Mother's Perfume

The second story occurred much later in Nicole's life. She was living at another house altogether long after graduating high school and, very sadly, after her mother had died. She and a friend were cleaning the house, particularly in the living room, when Nicole looked up at a painting of her mother that used to hang in the old house. She and her friend talked about the painting a bit, as the hurt of loss was still fresh in Nicole's heart, as indeed, it still is today. It was then, as they stood and remembered, that a smell rose up in the air, overtaking the antiseptic smells of cleaners and carpet powder. Nicole noticed it and asked her friend if she smelled it too. Her friend did indeed and asked Nicole what she thought it was. Nicole paused a moment taking it in and said,

"It's my mom. That is what she always smelled like." And then the smell was gone, lingering only long enough to make its presence known. Nicole has held on to this since as the final act of comfort her mom provided, a momentary return to let her know that she was still around, still there for her when needed.

Investigator's comments

Katie

I love this story from Patrick's friend. Having lost my own mother at roughly the same age, I understand the impact that such an encounter can have, and it reminds me of yet another experience that I had: It was the morning following my mother's death, and a knock came at the door of my parents' house. I am not sure why I answered it, but reason tends to dissipate in the immediacy of such a loss. Standing before me was an African-American woman, dressed in black from head to toe, and her style of clothing was oddly out of place. She gestured to me, and I said, "Now is really not a good time, could you come back another day?" She gave me a knowing smile and stated simply, "I have to give you something." Reluctantly, I opened the security door and, without saying another word, she handed me a small religious tract with a cover that read *Life in a Peaceful New World*. I can remember the numbness that came over me as the experience registered in my brain. As I looked up, she began to walk away, and I looked again at the paper in my hands. I looked out the door to see if I could see her, and she was gone. I looked up and down the street for her, but I never saw her again. Though it's been almost fifteen years since that happened, I still consider it a great source of comfort and assurance.

‡‡‡‡‡‡‡‡‡‡‡‡

The Sinister Grin

Patrick

As the stories in this book will show, houses are not the only private residences that can be haunted. Often the apartment is shouldered roughly out of the way by the more traditional and iconic vision of the haunted house with the overgrown yard and ramshackle fence. Apartments usually feel clean and safe and their proximity to other people gives the illusion of ethereal sterility. Aside from that, the age of some complexes make some people believe that they are simply not old enough to have ever had anything happen in them. None of these assertions are necessarily true.

Given the sheer number of people living in a relatively concentrated area, it's not difficult to see how apartment buildings would lend themselves to a wealth of activity. Many people come in and out in an almost endless stream of energy and it's not much of a stretch to assume that at least some of that will leave a mark. And that's not even taking into consideration that people do die in apartments. Houses do not have any sort of exclusivity contract with death. So, any number of things can happen in an apartment complex, and frankly, given all of the people who live in them, probably do.

The apartment in question for this tale can be found on 22nd Street at Prudence Road. It's a decent enough place; the apartments and grounds are well tended and the apartments, in a general sense, all feel comfortable. Carrying a fifty-pound dresser up the stairs to the second floor does challenge this notion slightly, but that is neither here nor there and is certainly not exclusive to this complex.

Once again, we revisit our friend, Nicole, who lived in the apartment with what became something of a revolving door of roommates. The apartment was the center of much activity as it was a hangout spot for a group of friends, myself included. Nicole lived in the apartment for a year and during that time many people either lived there or spent the night as a procession of friends and their significant others filtered in and out of the place.

It wasn't long into her occupancy when Nicole started noticing things were not as they should be. As is typical with most activity, there wasn't a wide variety, but rather a large volume of the same things over and over. The first thing she noticed was the voice that would call her name. The voice, presented as a female voice, would happen mostly at night. The second, if the two can be separated, was the sound of creaking in the hallway. The sound is generally associated with footsteps, but in this instance, distinct steps were not heard...just the creaking. That is really enough, though, when you are alone in a place and no one should be causing such a creak.

The activity didn't stop at sounds, although those did persist throughout the year. The activity graduated to objects being manipulated, as chess pieces on a chessboard would move. At one point, around one or two in the morning, a vacuum turned itself on. Given there was no one else in the apartment other than Nicole and her roommates at the time, this was not at all normal. While the voices and creaking sounds were persistent, there were no other major appliances turning themselves on.

Guests and residents who found themselves in the back bedroom also reported a general creepy feeling back there... as if they were not alone. Further, when anyone opened the patio door and leaned out for fresh air, they reported feeling as if they were about to be pushed. These sorts of reports led to all manner of speculation regarding the former occupants of that room and what particular fate they may have met. No answers were ever forthcoming, but the feelings were so intense and persistent in that room that it made people uncomfortable to stay there. It was that sort of discomfort that led to guests sleeping out in the living room area as opposed to what became the guest room after Nicole's first roommate moved out. Such was the situation one night when a friend of mine and I were staying over and camped out in the living room for the night. The light was off, but we were still talking to one another. I was lying on my side, and I was looking directly down the hall. The lights were off and it was dark, but there was a high enough level of light to see where everything was.

As we talked, something caught my eye down the hallway, some sort of movement. My eye focused first on the glowing green light of the smoke detector, I think because it was the brightest object in my field of vision. Discarding that as the source of the movement, my eyes shifted downward and I saw the figure of a girl leaning out from the door of the back bedroom. Her hair was long and hung down from her head as she leaned, a smile fixed solidly on her face. She was smiling, but it wasn't a particularly happy or welcoming smile. My first thought was that perhaps it was Nicole leaning out of her bedroom, which was adjacent to that back room, but a quick inspection of her door found it closed with the sounds of snoring filtering through.

I sat up and looked at the girl for a moment and decided I would say nothing about it, as it was probably just my mind playing tricks on me. That was when I heard my friend behind me say, "Who is THAT?" I reflexively gasped and got up and ran down the hall toward the bedroom, the girl darting back into the room. I turned on the light and looked everywhere in the room, but found it empty of any such smiling girls. After being satisfied that there was nothing in the room, I went back and eventually went to sleep. My friend and I didn't talk much about it that night. Still, she told Nicole the next day what had happened and her story, which was undiluted by anything I had said, mirrored my experience.

A Malfunction or the Paranormal?

The Phantom Elevator

Schools are one of the most frustrating sorts of haunted places to hear about. Because of the obvious safety risks, investigators can't go traipsing into a school whenever they please during the day while class is in session and the places are locked up at night tighter than a pawn shop in a bad part of town. So, you tend to hear a lot about schools being haunted, but rarely do you ever get to go or even get a lot of solid information about it. There are a lot of schools in Tucson that are alleged to be haunted but, again, there is not much by way of actual firsthand accounts. The next couple of stories, however, are tales from one person's experiences.

Randy, now a professional in the mental health field, at one point spent some time working as a custodian for various places, one of which was a school. As with most cleaning crews, Randy's shift put him there at night with a crew of two other guys. Randy had not been working at that particular school for long, but the other two were something of veterans of the location, having each been there for several years.

One particular night, the crew was ready to leave. It was 10 p.m. and Randy and one of the other custodians were standing at the open alarm box waiting for the third man to put away his keys. As they stood there in the dark of the school hallways, waiting to activate the alarm, they noticed something strange: the elevator was coming down. From the indicator, the elevator was coming down from the third floor. This was odd not only because they were the only three who were supposed to be in the building and none of them were on the third floor, but also

58

because in order to gain access to the elevator at all one would need a key. So the suggestion became that some third (or fourth, I suppose) party had access to a key and was traveling down the elevator.

Randy and the other man stood and watched for the doors to open, somewhat apprehensive about the occupant, but still fully expecting a person of the corporeal variety to be waiting on the other side of the doors. As the doors slid open, however, they found themselves staring at an empty chamber. As the new kid on the block, Randy was not so fazed by this and tried a reasonable explanation.

"So, is it supposed to do that? Like is that an every night at 10:07 thing?"

"Hell no!" said Randy's fellow custodian, who had many more years in the school than Randy and apparently did not take this in as much stride as Randy had.

The third man had joined them by this time, coming from the floor they were on, and it was decided that they would need to make a sweep of the building to see if someone was pulling an elaborate hoax on them. They each took a stairwell and moved up the floors, systematically checking all the classrooms on each floor.

After an exhaustive search, they had to conclude that they were the only ones in the building. Randy was still not nearly as freaked out by all of this as his compatriots, but the two senior staffers were not at all mellow about the incident. They were both scared to the point of having literal goose bumps on them and were very visibly shaken. Randy asked them if anything like that had ever happened before and they both confirmed that it had not. In his remaining time working the location, Randy never experienced anything at all like that again.

Investigator's comments

As obvious of a conclusion as it may be, it seems like this falls into the poltergeist category. Now, things flying around the room or otherwise being manipulated may not be what a person considers run-of-the-mill in a general sense, but in terms of having some sort of a fantastical explanation of some spectral prankster having a laugh on some unsuspecting janitors, this one just falls flat into the "it was probably one of them doing it without knowing it" category.

A lot of people, I think, really want there to be more to a story like this. As frightening of a proposition as it is, people want activity of this type to be of a grand scope. They want the horror movies to be real—and they want ghosts to be able to launch Machiavellian plots to scare the bejeezus out of people, but sadly, for those people of the more sensational variety, this simply does not seem to be the case.

From my experience and study of the subject, it seems like there is one of two things going on here. One — and this is the sort of explanation that sells books and increases TV ratings (despite not featuring a blue ringed trickster) — that one of the custodians somehow made the elevator descend and open with some unconscious, unleashed PK energy. The second, alternate explanation is so often overlooked in the zeal of an investigator wanting to proclaim some activity to be paranormal in nature, which is simply that the elevator was experiencing some sort of malfunction that brought it down and opened on its own.

Not being in the place and investigating it personally, this is one of those cases where a definitive ruling, elusive in the best of circumstances, is nearly impossible. While I have a difficult time imagining a scenario in which all the mechanisms that would keep an elevator from descending and opening on its own, completely free of the required key turns, could happen to fail all at the same time, it is at the very least possible—at least as possible as the alternative explanation. What is more compelling to me, however, is that two men who had worked there for years did not particularly put stock in the more mundane of the explanations. In a general sense, when you are in this sort of situation in a place you have been for years and completely absent of any occurrence like this in the past, and you are in a more repair-oriented field, ghosts are not the first culprit you go to. For these men to disregard a malfunction explanation suggests an added unlikelihood to that scenario that I may be unaware of regarding the operation of an elevator. So I am more inclined to side with them that this was something really, really strange.

While I can't say for certain, it would appear that there was something on one of the custodians' minds that night and it caused him to let go of some PK that made the elevator drop and open. Though whatever caused it was fleeting, as it didn't occur again. Whatever the explanation, this sort of strange incident certainly flies in the face of any description of late-night custodial work at a school being boring and uneventful.

‡‡‡‡‡‡‡‡‡‡‡‡

Vacuum Blues

We've established that grade schools are often untapped resources for paranormal activity given they are usually more active than a retail store on Black Friday and roughly as accessible as Area 51. It's frustrating for investigators to be aware of hotbeds of activity and be completely off limits to them. Thankfully, college campuses share the same proclivity for paranormal activity and have the added accessibility that the over-eighteen crowd provides. The University of Arizona is no exception.

Centennial Hall on the University of Arizona campus is a fine venue and home to all manner of productions from ballet, plays, stand-up comedy, and orchestral concerts. The Hall sees thousands of people in its seats every year. It also carries with it rumors of being haunted, suggesting that the patrons filling the seats are not the only inhabitants of the theater.

As it happens, our janitor Randy also worked as a custodian during college at Centennial Hall. Randy worked the morning

Centennial Hall, University of Arizona

shift from 4 a.m. to noon, but one night he was called in early at 2 a.m. He didn't have keys and had to be let into the building. Upon entering, he found himself completely alone in the theater. The other custodian who had been called in was working in another building and the supervisor who let him in was elsewhere.

So it was just Randy...vacuuming the theater in a darkened auditorium when nature called. Randy turned off the vacuum and left it to go take care of business. Upon his return, he found the vacuum had not only been turned back on, but had now migrated as far away as it could go without pulling the cord. Now, had the vacuum not been on and been parked on an incline, it would have been easy to imagine something so mundane as it rolling down the aisle. But, in this case, not only had it *rolled* away for no apparent reason, it had been turned on as well. Of course, someone could have played a prank by sneaking into the hall, turning the vacuum on, and moving it several feet from its resting place, but in this particular instance, that scenario was highly unlikely.

The place was locked from all sides and the only person who had the keys was Randy's supervisor, who not only had no sense of humor whatsoever, but also would have made a great deal of noise coming through the door. The Hall, designed to carry sound, echoed enormously and the sounds of the doors opening was not something easily missed. Couple that with the fact that the bathroom was only a short distance from the vacuum's location and the fact that Randy was only gone a few seconds and you have something out of the ordinary.

Randy was aware that the place was said to be haunted, so he told a co-worker the story and unsurprisingly, the co-worker turned completely white and exclaimed that the same thing had happened to him. He went on to tell Randy that there were two ghosts that were supposed to haunt the place; one was said to be a sad, young girl and the other, a playful old man who had died of a heart attack.

Randy never experienced anything else at the Hall, but another co-worker told him of an incident when he was walking across the stage and heard a second set of footsteps following closely behind him. He increased his pace and the footsteps followed suit until the man finally sprinted his way to the other side and jumped off the stage.

These stories are not at all unique for the theater and, at least for the custodial crew, apparently the performances don't necessarily stop when the shows are over. As with many old theaters around the country, Centennial Hall is the sort of place that patrons hate to leave—and apparently don't.

Investigator's comments

The activity described is interesting in that you have mischievous pranks being played on workers in the form of moved objects, but don't seem to have any kind of a constant agent to pin the PK on. As mentioned previously, the source of poltergeist activity is widely considered to be a person doing it unconsciously. But, as with anything paranormal, the rules are not hard and fast and it's not outside the realm of possibility that a sentient entity like an apparition could use the same PK that a living agent might use and affect objects in space. While that isn't scientifically supported in a general sense, there are a proliferation of cases in which a constant agent is not present, yet objects are manipulated anyway. So on a best educated guess basis, it's not unreasonable to conclude that a mischievous spirit could learn to manipulate objects. In the case of the roving, self-starting vacuum, the above theory seems to be the best explanation, outside of some large-scale, well-organized prank campaign leveled squarely against Randy. In this case, "ghosts moving stuff" sounds about right.

Demonic Specters?

Scary Laundry

It's generally accepted amongst professionals, particularly on the science side of this study, that apparitions cannot hurt you. They are generally not attributed with the ability to affect objects or really insinuate themselves into the physical world in any meaningful way beyond speech or appearance. Not everyone agrees with this assessment, but the consensus is definitely that object manipulation is the arena of unconscious PK energy as opposed to the apparition. However, while an apparition may not have the overt ability to do harm, it is still quite able to fill you with fear, dread, and uneasiness. As this next story demonstrates, even in the absence of overt physical effects, an apparition can still make you feel like you are in danger. As with so many of these stories, the activity doesn't offer much variety, but makes up for that in consistency.

For Mila, there was always something about the laundry room in the house in which she grew up. Not really something bad necessarily, but just something sort of odd. As a young girl, the curiosity remained just that given she had little business in the room on a day-to-day basis. As she got older and found herself taking over her own laundry duties in high school, this would all change.

She began to do her own laundry and over time she started to feel strange. She disregarded these feelings as abject silliness and dismissed them out of hand. She believed all she would have to do is acknowledge that she was spooking herself out and it would go away, but as time went on, the feelings were much too pervasive to ignore. The more time she spent in there the more convinced she became that something was just not right.

Mila, like so many of us, has trouble sleeping at night. Sure, it's not some widespread plague, but insomnia is a fairly common affliction and seems to precipitate paranormal activity if only because a person is up at the appropriate hour for most odd things to be going on. In this case, the appropriate hour was any time after midnight. As she did her laundry at night, because she was not sleeping anyway and the placement of the laundry room to the rest of the house made this an unobtrusive practice, she found that after 12 a.m., strange things would start to happen. Mila tested her theory by doing the laundry at different times both before and after the 12 a.m. deadline and found that as long as she was done before midnight, she was hunky dory. If, however, she exceeded the deadline, it became a matter of hurrying up and getting the heck out of Dodge.

It started out small. She would go in and begin her laundry and as the hands on the clock slid past 12, she would have a distinct feeling of weight on her as if something was pressing in. At this stage, it did not feel particularly threatening or malicious; it was just there and hadn't been before. Certainly odd, but nothing to be particularly alarmed about in a general sense. Had it ended there, it would have been no big deal, and would not have been cause to flee. Of course, it did not.

Within several moments of the initial activity, the weight graduated into full-scale dread. In Mila's own words, "[It's] like death is looming, and there's something there that very much wants to cause it." No matter which way she turned or what she did in the room, the feeling pressed in on her, always from behind...the weight now carrying with it the malevolent feeling of impending harm. There was nothing at all she could do to make the feeling of something behind her go away, and the need to move reached a fever pitch that stayed with her until she was well out of the room and behind a closed door. She found absolutely nothing could be done to make the feelings go away in the room itself. Only fleeing to another part of the house and closing a door would return any feeling of safety.

Over the years, friends and family have experienced the same feelings in the laundry room after midnight. Some experienced it blindly and some were told beforehand. A good many were people who didn't believe and went in to try to disprove such a ridiculous notion—only to return with reports of experiencing the activity as described. There were two guests who had somewhat unique experiences that are worth mentioning specifically.

The first involves Mila's friend, Nathan, who was unique amongst the skeptics that she had run across because he was firm in his belief that it was absolute hornswoggle, but at the same time abjectly refused to go in there after the alleged witching hour. It was only after a spirited round of daring that he finally agreed to do it despite his assertion that he was no longer five years old and dares had no power over him.

He happened to be over watching a movie one night, not long after Mila's 22nd birthday, when she saw that it was well past the haunting hour and she engaged in the hallowed "I dare you" ritual. After the aforementioned disclaimer that he was impervious to such immature maneuvering, he agreed to go. As he made his way down the hallway toward the laundry room, he paused in hesitation. Mila offered to let him opt out of his dare, but he refused, saying he was going to do it. After gathering himself, he went into the laundry room alone.

If staying in the laundry room was an endurance test, he would have failed hands down as he fled the room just moments after entering and immediately fled to the relative safety of the bathroom and shut the door, most likely because of Mila's missives about getting behind a door. When he exited the bathroom, shaken, he told Mila that it had been just as she described except that there was no lag time between weight and terror. It all came on him at once and he was forced to flee immediately. He became, from then on, a believer in the story and another skeptic to be turned by the formidable power of the laundry room.

The second odd story doesn't directly involve the laundry room, but rather the bathroom down the hall. Mila's younger cousin was over and tended to be a bit more shaky and fearful than most, so Mila never mentioned any manner of strangeness to her. All the same, her cousin encountered strangeness that was at once amusing and terrifying. It also seemingly flies in the face of our earlier assertions about what an apparition can and cannot do.

She had been down visiting from Phoenix and was staying the night at Mila's. They were up late, and she needed to go to the bathroom. Thinking nothing of it, she did just that, going to the one closest to the laundry room. Mila also thought it was no big deal; after all, going to the bathroom is pretty much standard operating procedure. As Mila sat there waiting for her to come back, she heard the telltale signs of someone finishing up and heard her cousin burst out of the bathroom all at once giggling hysterically. When she returned to the room Mila was in, however, her face wore an expression of horror as opposed to glee.

It took several moments for Mila to calm her cousin down enough to find out what was going on. Apparently, according to her cousin, she had not been responsible for either the toilet flushing or the sink turning on. On top of that, she hadn't even made it to the toilet in the first place. She had been on her way to the facilities when the toilet flushed and the sink turned on by itself. The toilet flushed first and, as she turned to flee, the sink went on full blast. Mila got up to go inspect the scene and found the water to still be on.

These are just two stories of many that tell the tale of Mila's laundry room, a facility that even now does more than soak out stains and brighten brights. Consistency, as always, is key and this place has it. Sure a laundry room isn't the first place you think of when you think of hauntings, but things can happen anywhere and besides, a ghost needs a place to wash its sheets.

Investigator's Comments

Obviously the more sensational stories that everyone wants to read about are going to be of the "I saw a ghost" or "that coffee pot just levitated in the air and dumped coffee on Dad's head" category, but the ones that tend to be the scariest are the ones in which you see nothing at all, but are left with a feeling. In the laundry room stories, we see that in play. There doesn't have to be something overt and in-your-face—and very often there is not.

When investigating, your feelings and reactions to a location are often the most important tool available. Whether you consider yourself to be a sensitive, or just someone who can discern the noteworthy from the mundane, how an area feels is usually the best indication of activity, or at least is a worthy jumping-off point for further study. I would never claim to be "sensitive," but I am fairly well attuned to what is normal and what is not, and what might be noteworthy. In this case, given the pervasive feelings that stretch across believers and non-believers alike, I think there is a good chance that something may very well be going on here.

On the other hand, when dealing with feelings (particularly when a story is well known), there becomes an issue with the power of suggestion. If you know you're expected to feel a certain way, you often will. That is the reason for the blind methodologies in investigations. If you don't know what to feel, then your feelings are far more valid. In some of the examples given above, people expected a certain feeling and the fact that they had them really doesn't prove or disprove the presence of something out of the ordinary.

Still, given the incidents in which there was no prior knowledge involved, I lean toward believing the activity to be legitimate, especially given the absolute trustworthiness of the storyteller in this case. As an investigator, however, you do always need to look for the normal explanations first before even approaching the paranormal ones. You want to protect your credibility at all times and false positives are never a good thing.

A Visit from the Reaper

Katie

During the course of organizing this book, I must have asked the question "Have you got any ghost stories?" approximately 10,000 times. About 9,999 times, the answer is, "No. Sorry." Once in a while, though, you find someone who says, "Holy crap, DO I have a ghost story!" Such was the case with my brother-in-law, Christopher. Christopher is a nurse and he was working in a local hospital at the time of his experience. Assigned to his charge was a patient who had a notorious history for being mean to staff and for possessing a generally evil demeanor and hateful disposition. Now, most people who are described as "mean" or "hateful" are by and large just misunderstood, socially awkward individuals who would rather take a beating than have to interact with other people. For the most part, they wish no ill will on anyone. Once in a blue moon, however, you meet someone who may just be the exception to that rule. Even rarer still is the happenstance that would allow one to be present during such an individual's final moments on earth.

Christopher had been making his normal rounds, tending to his patients in the relative calm of the hospital ward. The female patient in question had been in failing health for some time and was in and out of consciousness as a result. This evening — which would ultimately be her last — she awoke from her unconscious state and began screaming. According to Christopher, these were not the run-of-the-mill screams that are common enough in a hospital floor filled with people of various pain tolerance levels. These were the type of blood-curdling screams one might emit just before taking a hatchet to the sternum. Christopher hurried to the room to see the patient sitting upright in her bed, staring at the foot of it and screaming,

"They're coming for me!" Normally, one would take such an outburst as the confused ramblings of someone suffering from severe dementia, and steps would be taken to calm the patient — be it by a soothing lullaby or sedating Thorazine. Here is where the story differs: Christopher entered the room to find a dark, shadowy figure moving towards the bed, wrapping itself around her feet as she lay screaming. Her screams only lasted a few moments before she died, the horrified look still frozen on her face, illustrating the sheer terror that welcomed her into her afterlife. Christopher was the only living soul to witness her deeply disturbing end and he describes it as the "creepiest thing" he's ever seen.

Investigator's comments

Even as a seasoned paranormal investigator, there are some things that I find particularly disturbing, the biggest thing being any contact with anything that might even remotely be demonic. I am sure that everyone has heard stories of near-death experiences in which the patient in question experiences being out of his own body, walking towards a bright light, and feeling an enormous sense of love and warmth and happiness. Often, these people say that they wanted to go into the light, but a voice tells them to go back, that it is not yet their time. What people hear far less are the near-death experiences that are not as positive and loving. When someone has this type of experience, it is described as a feeling of complete, abject terror coupled with the feeling of having one's soul torn apart by dark, faceless creatures not unlike those portrayed in the movie "Ghost."

I suppose the lesson here is to straighten up and fly right. We don't really KNOW what awaits us when we die, but clearly there IS some manner of afterlife.

The Ghost of Fort Lowell

During the course of researching this book, we have relied on the good graces of many people to get some of the ghost stories that may not be as well known, but are as interesting as they are frightening. One such story came to us from Judy Ciampoli, president of the Old Fort Lowell Neighborhood Association. Attached to her email was a scanned image of an old, yellowed newspaper article written by Don Schellie, discussing the rock-throwing ghost of Fort Lowell.

Rock-throwing?

Yes, rock-throwing.

According to legend, the first reports of the ghost surfaced around the turn of last century, not terribly long after the Fort had been abandoned. By that time, the fort had fallen into disrepair, although a small settlement had established itself in the area. When the ghost turned up for the first time, there were plenty of people around to see it, according to the newspapers of the day. In the Schellie article, he mentions that witnesses described the ghost as being of "unusual stature" and also being dressed as a soldier.

As eyewitness reports of ghost sightings increased, so did the general sense of discomfort of the residents. When the ghost began appearing on an almost daily basis in December of 1900, the citizens hatched a plan to get to the bottom of this "phantom soldier" business, once and for all. In a rather spectacular display, the townsfolk waited until he appeared and began blasting their guns at the phantom while simultaneously releasing the neighborhood dogs to give chase.

Although well-organized, the affront was to no avail. The phantom simply vanished into thin air. On several subsequent occasions, the townspeople attempted to run him down, each time ending with the mysterious disappearance of the interloper. This pattern of Scooby-Doo-esque investigation continued for an uncertain length of time until, finally, the

Fort Lowell - home to the infamous rock-throwing ghost.

phantom soldier had his fill. During a close pursuit of the specter, one citizen was surprised to be assaulted by an arsenal of stones hurled at him by the ghost as – once again – the soldier disappeared. It has been a very long time since the last reported sighting of the apparition, but the legend continues to this day. Perhaps the ghost became tired of the constant pursuit, and has decided to spend his eternity below the paranormal radar.

Investigator's comments

By today's standards of paranormal investigation, this story is just about as fantastic as it gets. Quite frankly, I find it refreshing to hear a ghost story that doesn't result in an entire family being too terrified to live in their own home. This is almost as scary as being chased by a ghost holding a rubber chicken. In this case, though, I think I'm more inclined to feel sad for the ghost than frightened for the townsfolk. Although one might be very quick to dismiss this tale as an example of mass hysteria, numerous reports by otherwise reputable citizens have kept this bit of local lore alive for over a century. This ghost may have just been going about his business, but his presence became enough of a menace that an entire community joined forces in an attempt to rid themselves of the spectral soldier. This case certainly gives a new take on the phrase "ghost hunt."

‡‡‡‡‡‡‡‡‡‡‡‡‡

A Plethora of Ghosts

When I told my friend Linda that I was collecting ghost stories, she immediately said to me, "Did I ever tell you what happened in Marana?" Marana is located on the northwest edge of Tucson. In recent years, this community has seen an upsurge in popularity and is slowly becoming one of Tucson's more high-end zip codes for retirees and Phoenix commuters. Prior to its "discovery," Marana was known more for its isolation from the heart of Tucson and was more popular with people seeking to live in the "middle of nowhere." There were also abundant rumors of Marana being a haven for satanic rituals. Now, in all fairness, I know of no instance where those rumors were ever substantiated and I am inclined to say that they were just a product of teenage gossip. That being said, the experiences relayed to me by my good friend would give pause to anyone quick to dismiss those rumors.

Linda had been living in her mother-in-law's manufactured home along with her husband, Mick, and two sons, who were both under the age of three. It was definitely not her first choice to impose upon her husband's family, but it was during the salad days of marriage when decisions were made based on financial hardship rather than personal comfort. She had never felt particularly comfortable living so far off the beaten path, and she found that being alone in the house often left her feeling very "on edge." Sometimes she would see figures moving out of the corner of her eye, but would dismiss it as an overactive imagination. One evening, however, she had her first experience that made her realize that she may not be imagining any of it. She had been in the bathroom washing her face, when she was suddenly aware of the sound of someone walking into the bathroom (now, in a manufactured home there is no mistaking someone's approach because you can not only hear the sound, but you can feel the movement in the floor). While rinsing her face, she could see the floor behind her and she saw — and felt — a pair of men's feet walking into the bathroom. She stood up and looked in the mirror, expecting to see her husband behind her, and was very surprised to see that no one was in the room with her. With her heart rate slightly elevated, she set out to find Mick and read him the riot act for trying to scare her. When she found him, he was in another room watching television. The interrogation went something like this:

Linda says insistently, "Honey, did you just come into the bathroom when I was washing my face?"

His reply, without taking his eyes from the television, "No."

Linda now has one hand on her hip and the other weakly gesturing towards the bathroom, "Are you sure, because I saw you walk into the bathroom?"

His gaze now turns to her and he states very matter-of-factly, "Well, you couldn't have seen me walk into the bathroom because I have been right here watching TV."

Quickly shifting her weight from one leg to the other, she pleads. "Come on, honey. It's not funny."

He shrugs his shoulders and holds his hands out. "I didn't do anything!"

She glares impatiently.

He insists, "I swear to you that I haven't moved from this spot since you went in there."

The sincerity in his voice convinced her that he had, in fact, not gone into the bathroom and there was no one else home with them at the time. She put the incident out of her mind and decided not to mention it again.

Not long after that happened, Linda found herself alone with her two children while the rest of the household was visiting relatives nearby. Her oldest son was confined to his room with a baby gate, and the baby was in a carrier to allow her to finish the dishes before anyone returned home. With her back to the front of the house, Linda heard the front door open and then slam shut, and she turned to see a man she didn't recognize wearing a red shirt and blue jeans look over his shoulder at her as he hurriedly walked down the hall. As he passed by her son's bedroom, the child began screaming. She immediately ran to the back of the house (hoping beyond all hope that it was just her husband and that her eyes were playing tricks on her) with the expectation of finding her husband in the bedroom. Instead, she rushed into the back bedroom to find it dark, empty, and *very, very* cold. Afraid that someone may be hiding in the back of the house, she gathered her children and called her husband, who immediately rushed home. An inspection of the rest of the house yielded nothing, but as he entered the bedroom, Linda's husband stopped in his tracks: the bathroom door that he had closed before leaving was standing open, and the light was on. Linda had not entered the back bedroom except to investigate the man in the red shirt, and even then the room had been completely dark. It would have been impossible not to notice the bright light streaming from the bathroom.

At this point, Linda, who is deeply religious and of unshakable faith, decided it best to put herself on a "high alert" and felt compelled to rid the house of anything she deemed questionable in spiritual content. Specifically focusing on some record albums left behind by her brother-in-law, she asked Mick to dispose of them in the outside trash bin. After much coaxing and cajoling, he finally relented and one evening he carried them to the dumpster. As he was loading them, Linda stood in the doorway and insisted that he not just dispose of them, but he first destroy them. He somewhat reluctantly obliged, and began breaking the albums and throwing them away. As Linda oversaw the process, she became aware of a very large dog emerge from the dark desert, approaching Mick as he destroyed the contraband. The dog walked up to Mick and stood directly in his line of sight and remained there for several minutes before walking away. Linda watched nervously from the top of the exterior steps and wondered why Mick had done nothing to scare off the mangy beast. As the dog walked past, it strode in front of the house, turned to Linda and looked her right in the eyes, and continued down the dirt road in the opposite direction from where it emerged from the shadows. When Mick finished his task and returned to the house, Linda impatiently asked why he had so cavalierly ignored the big, strange dog that could so easily have bitten him. His response was simply, "What dog?" Now, clearly at the end of her tether, Linda insisted, "The dog that was standing right next to you, watching you smash the records!" His response was a very predictable, "There was no dog standing next to me."

She relayed the entire story to Mick, and they both agreed that perhaps an alternate living arrangement would be appropriate. Not long after, they packed up their glad rags and moved to an apartment in town, never to be bothered by ghostly man or beast again — for a little while, anyway.

They actually ended up moving a few times before settling into an apartment located on Fort Lowell (not too far from the stomping grounds of the rock-throwing ghost). By this time, they had a third child – a girl – and Linda definitely had her hands full. Not long after their daughter began walking and talking, she would tell her mother about the "stick figure people" who ran around in Linda's bedroom every night. Linda always thought this was the overactive imagination of a toddler, but I recently had the opportunity to ask her daughter about these "stick figure people."

Now thirteen years old, Linda's daughter can still recall with perfect clarity how these small, dark apparitions made her lay awake in her bed, afraid, on a daily basis. She described them as being shaped like the people on restroom doors, and they would emerge from her mother's closet every night. Although they never specifically bothered Linda's daughter, they would wreak havoc on the bedroom by moving objects and opening drawers. Linda's daughter kept herself awake at night wondering what would happen if they started coming into her room and bothering her.

Now, the description of these apparitions may sound cute, but keep in mind that kids have an uncanny ability to see and hear things that adults have been programmed to tune out. What she describes is eerily similar to many reports of apparitions (and even a little poltergeist activity), but the description from a three-year-old's perspective is the simplest one that her mind can conjure. Linda has even admitted to being scared in that bedroom on more than one occasion, and admits to having recurring dreams of being shot in her bed. Upon relaying this information to Mick, he admitted that prior to moving into the apartment, the manager disclosed to him that someone had been murdered there some time ago, but he didn't tell her because he knew she would be scared.

Investigator's comments

Unless present at the time of the incident, it becomes very difficult to verify reports of people being murdered in apartments. It's not like one can call the manager and say, "Oh, hey, yeah...I was just wondering, was anyone ever MURDERED in your apartment complex?" and unless you are a prospective tenant, they aren't just going to offer up such scandal — especially if you are going to publish it in a book about haunted places. I WILL submit that this particular apartment complex is not a place I would want to find myself after dark, and I surely wouldn't be SURPRISED to learn that someone had met an untimely and unfortunate end within its confines. That being said, it's not too big of a stretch to imagine that Linda and her family found themselves living with a little ethereal residue. Additionally, in this situation (and, likely, the stories provided by Nicole Perdue) we have a scenario where a group of people experienced numerous occurrences in varied locations. This illustrates the belief that certain people are more sensitive to paranormal activity, much in the same way that some people are allergic to cats, and it can seem as though the activity is following them. Although it's possible for an individual to be followed by an entity, it is more likely that multiple and varied experiences simply indicate a genetic predisposition towards paranormal sensitivity.

As of this writing, Linda, Mick, and their family reside in a lovely, eastside home — completely free of any paranormal activity.

Uninvited Ghosts

All in the Family

As I mentioned, paranormal activity has a tendency to "run in the family," so it's no surprise then that my sister would have her own set of experiences to bring to the table. When her oldest child – now in his twenties – was a toddler, she lived in a small, unassuming ranch-style home on the east side of Tucson. The house did not have a colorful past, or a particularly creepy countenance, but it did give her a couple of serious frights. As she lay sleeping one night, she opened her eyes to find an older woman dressed in a high-collared, long-sleeved prairie-style dress, her grey hair in a loose bun atop her head, glaring down at my sister from the foot of her bed. Frozen with fear, she could not muster the effort or the sound to awaken her significant other. As this woman continued to glower wickedly at her, my sister finally gathered the wherewithal to reach across the bed and turn on the lamp, expecting the light to wash away the frightening image. Instead what happened was a loud popping noise and a shower of broken glass as the light bulb exploded with no cause or provocation. Understandably terrified, she finally managed to wake her boyfriend, who very bravely got out of bed and turned on a different light. She described what happened and he looked at her like she was insane. The scary old lady never returned, and whatever foreboding message she was trying to deliver was eventually lost in the chaotic shuffle of life.

My sister often worked overnight shifts, and was a frequent day sleeper. As such, anything that people with a regular circadian rhythm would consider normal would often cause a significant disruption to her sleep schedule. For example, a landlord wishing to have a few repairs made to the home during the day would generally be something that would have to be scheduled far enough in advance to guarantee that she would be awake and not deprived of sleep for her next shift. So imagine her annoyance at being awakened during the middle of her sleep to a workman beginning to do repairs in her home. Upon opening her eyes, she looked across the hall to find said workman, complete with a yellow construction hat, who had apparently let himself into her home, was now taking measurements of the doorframe. Ruling out the possibility that it was her boyfriend, she called out to the man, "Hello? Can I help you?" but was ignored. Once the workman finished taking the measurements, he simply vanished into thin air.

No explanation was ever available as to the "who" and "why" of the occurrences that happened to her in that home. Nothing else out of the ordinary ever happened, at least not that anyone shared with her, and no research into the history of the home was ever done to establish why these two totally unrelated and incongruous events happened to begin with. She has long since moved out of that house, but still remembers these bizarre events with perfect clarity.

Investigator's comments

One might argue that my sister was simply dreaming these two images, since both occurred immediately as she awakened from sleep. The strange thing in this case — and the thing that suggests that these events were a product of some sort of tear in the delicate veil that separates the living from the dead — is the duration that both events lasted. Normally, if something is seen during sleep, the image vanishes as soon as the sleeper awakens. This was not the case. She was awake several minutes for both experiences, and she also experienced a bit of poltergeist-type activity when the light bulb exploded. This is another sparkling example of just how ordinary the extraordinary becomes when paranormal activity camouflages itself in the background of a normal day in suburbia.

Haunted Hospital

Hospitals, by and large, are great places for paranormal activity. It's no surprise then that one hospital on the south side of Tucson has at least one resident ghost of its own causing all sorts of commotion. As the story goes, there was once a patient undergoing psychiatric treatment in the hospital and was so distraught and overwhelmed with life that he chose to end his own by leaping from an upper-floor window, landing on some loading docks below (if not that, then he just took an unplanned and unfortunate spill). Regardless of how, exactly, the events panned out, the loss of life is very tragic. It becomes very intriguing that the deceased seems to have decided to stick around a while, particularly in the area of the shipping department, near where his body was allegedly recovered.

Ray, an employee of the shipping department, explained that, although he is not sure exactly how the events leading to the ghostly experiences unfolded, he is certain there is something there. The activity he describes includes the quite common sensation that someone (or something) is tugging on the shirts or pant legs of many of the employees, and – just as often – the sound of a whispering voice saying "hey," in an effort to get someone's attention. A quick look around the department confirms that no living beings are responsible for the ghostly salutation. Lending to the rumors of a haunting is an automatic, motion-sensing door that leads to the department and is known to open and close of its own accord...often when there is no corporeal motion to trip the sensor.

The last thing that Ray describes as a frequent occurrence happens when leaving the restroom. On several occasions he has exited the room, turning out the lights as he leaves, only to find that someone has turned the lights back on immediately after he has left the restroom, even when he is the only one in the department. Obviously, something is trying to get his attention, even if only to acknowledge its existence.

Investigator's comments

As a paranormal researcher, I have come to the personal and professional opinion that every hospital is haunted. No other category of real estate has seen more death behind its collective walls than hospitals, and – generally speaking – death inside of a hospital is usually surrounded by trauma and despair. Nobody is ever HAPPY to go to the hospital (outside of childbirth) and people are programmed not to expect a positive outcome. Very often, people who die in hospitals were, only hours or moments ago, sitting in their living room watching TV, or crossing the street, or driving home from work. They had no idea that today would be their last day on Earth, and they certainly did not make any specific plans for entry into the afterlife. I am only guessing here (and I certainly have no immediate plans for finding out), but it seems like dying – without the benefit of prior knowledge and expectation – might be more than just a little confusing. If everything that we have been taught is true, the spirit continues seamlessly into the afterlife. This could mean that one second you are sitting up comfortably, eating green Jello, and the next you are standing by your bedside wondering why everyone is so upset. Ergo, you have no idea that you are dead. You are blissfully unaware of your demise, and thrilled at how good you feel. Based on this scenario, it could explain why so many souls are just wandering around in the last place they were alive. No one will answer their questions. The family has stopped visiting. The doctor no longer stops by on his rounds… They just don't know to leave.

Downtown Tucson

Something's Fishy

Downtown Tucson is filled with historic homes and buildings dating back well over a century. One such property located off of 12th Street seems to have an unseen occupant that may be as old as the dwelling. Originally built in 1883, this adorable apartment home – now part of a triplex – is currently occupied by Cassandra and William, who noticed almost right away that they may not be the only ones residing in the space.

Cassandra describes it as, "At night, it feels like there is someone there."

Agreeing with Cassandra, William adds, "The air in the bedroom gets thick at night."

Now, to the uninitiated, this may sound like nothing more than a problem with the air circulation in the home, but that's just the beginning of the reported activity, which seems to focus around the bedroom.

Cassandra recalls one incident involving a statue of a small Egyptian cat that sits on the table in the bedroom. "I was sitting here, talking on the phone and lining it up [with the corner of the table]. I left, and when I came back, it was moved to the center of the table."

William further went on to say, "We never point it in that direction [facing the bed]; we always point it towards the door."

Cassandra also relayed another experience in which an item in a fishbowl seemed to move of its own accord. "We adore our fish and we talk to him all the time," she explained. Pointing to the decorative snake inside the bowl, she said, "The snake always faces out, but one day it was just turned around. We wouldn't have done that."

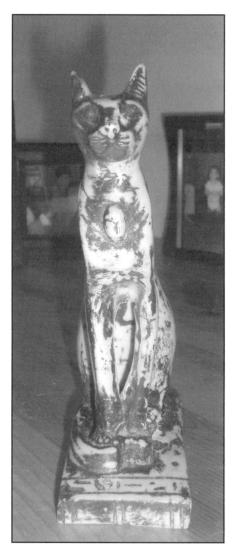

An Egyptian cat that moves of its own accord in Cassandra and William's townhouse.

Not only does the ghost seem to have a penchant for rearranging the bric-a-brac, but he also appears to enjoy opening the blinds and unlocking the window when no one is home. Additionally, the door that separates the bedroom from the kitchen has a tendency to open on its own, even though when closed, the door requires a bit of a shove to pop it open (an inspection of the door revealed no abnormality that would cause it to pop open and there is no detectable cross breeze that would account for the force necessary to open the door).

Cassandra even recalled one instance where she was in the bathtub and heard footsteps in the bedroom. Of course she was home alone. Each occurrence has resulted in a call to the landlord, only to find that he has not been around the property that day, and no one else has a key.

Investigator's comments

This type of activity perfectly demonstrates the reality of paranormal phenomena. It does not involve huge theatrics and

Hollywood-style effects, it just simply "is." Perhaps, however, the most disturbing aspect of this activity is the sense that someone has gained access into your personal home, and is manipulating your sanity by doing just enough to make you think you are losing your mind.

‡‡‡‡‡‡‡‡‡‡‡‡‡

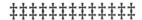

Unseen Audience

Downtown Tucson is a really strange blend of vintage architecture and contemporary style. Currently undergoing a long-needed revitalization, there are still many buildings in the downtown area which time seems to have simply forgotten. Sitting empty, they wait for Prince Charming and the glass slipper to transform them into either trendy condominiums with etched concrete floors, granite countertops, and a million dollar price tag, or the increasingly ubiquitous historically-significant-property-turned-law-offices. Until that time, there are still some buildings in the downtown area that have both historic interest and accessibility to regular folks...*and ghosts*.

One such building, located at 6th Avenue and Pennington Street, was once the home of Mountain Bell, and later, AT&T. In its most recent incarnation, the building is used as a rehearsal space where several local bands practice and store equipment between shows. The space has remained untouched since it was last occupied and, as evidenced, the glass case housing the mandatory postings of human resources material still proudly hangs in place, informing workers of the $3.35 minimum wage. It has also been rumored that this building was once used as a morgue, which might explain some of the strange goings-on.

I learned of this building through a coworker of mine, Melissa, who told me that her boyfriend has encountered some pretty freaky situations in the practice room. Given the nature of any local music scene, I immediately wondered exactly what type of activity would have to occur in order for the occupants to consider it freaky.

According to Melissa, it was around 3:30 a.m. and her boyfriend, Ray, was getting ready to leave after practicing his drums. As he was gathering his belongings, a water bottle sitting atop a television flew from where it was sitting and fell to the ground. Startled, he quickened his pace. Almost immediately following that incident, a stereo that had been sitting on top of a milk crate crashed to the ground with such force that it knocked over part of his drum set. Melissa described Ray as being "a little freaked out," so he grabbed what he could carry and beat a hasty retreat to his car. Unfortunately, the practice room is on the third floor, which meant three flights of stairs in a dark stairwell. Whatever was in the practice room with him must have wanted to

The stairwell of the rehearsal space where Ray was pushed by unseen hands.

make sure he left the building: "It felt like someone was pushing and forcing me down the stairs!" Ray recounted. As soon as he reached the exit, the door closed behind him with a deafening slam...especially interesting given that the large metal door is controlled by a hydraulic hinge, and was not malfunctioning in any way up to that point.

This is not the only time that weird things have happened to him in that building. At one point, the band was recording a demo. During the recording session, no transient noises were heard until the CD was played back, and the distinct sound of a person groaning could be heard. Not long after, the band upgraded some of its equipment including the microphones. These microphones are apparently so well made that they are able to pick up noises that are inaudible to the human ear. One night, while the band was taking a break from practicing, the microphones continued to pick up the sounds of voices, even though the band was not playing, and no other bands were in the building at the time. Not only are the microphones able to pick up the sounds of disembodied voices, they have also picked up the sound of someone tapping on the microphone, even with no one within arm's reach.

Investigator's Comments

I've said it so many times before...downtown Tucson is absolutely crawling with ghosts, whether we know about all of them or not. The energy is such a strange mixture of history meets modern, and the people who attract this energy are equally as eclectic. That type of atmosphere and its artistic and artful participants are often much more accepting of all types of people... *living or dead*. It would only be appropriate that this rehearsal space have a resident music critic making sure everyone keeps hitting the right notes.

Ghosts of the Sosa-Carrillo-Fremont House

Tucson is a very old city, and, occasionally, you can still find perfectly preserved pieces of its past. Such is the case with the Sosa-Carrillo-Fremont House, literally located in the middle of the convention center complex in downtown Tucson.

The house was built in the mid-1800s and was owned and occupied by several families over the years, hence the length of its name. Among its residents was Elizabeth Fremont, daughter of Arizona's fifth territorial governor, John C. Fremont, whose historical significance was what prevented this home from being razed (along with the rest of the neighborhood) in 1972, when the property was acquired to make way for the Tucson Convention Center. The home was completely restored, and is now appointed with period furnishings compliments of the Arizona Historical Society.

Sosa-Carrillo-Fremont House, Tucson Community Center.

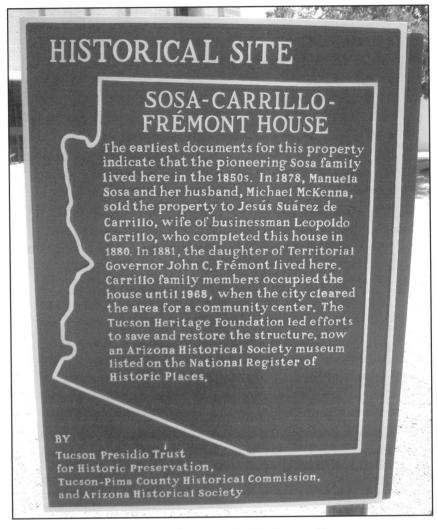

HISTORICAL SITE

SOSA-CARRILLO-FRÉMONT HOUSE

The earliest documents for this property indicate that the pioneering Sosa family lived here in the 1850s. In 1878, Manuela Sosa and her husband, Michael McKenna, sold the property to Jesús Suárez de Carrillo, wife of businessman Leopoldo Carrillo, who completed this house in 1880. In 1881, the daughter of Territorial Governor John C. Frémont lived here. Carrillo family members occupied the house until 1968, when the city cleared the area for a community center. The Tucson Heritage Foundation led efforts to save and restore the structure, now an Arizona Historical Society museum listed on the National Register of Historic Places.

BY
Tucson Presidio Trust
for Historic Preservation,
Tucson-Pima County Historical Commission,
and Arizona Historical Society

A plaque explaining the history of the Sosa-Carrillo-Fremont House.

The house also appears to still boast some of its original occupants.

We visited the Sosa-Carrillo-Fremont House recently, and were greeted by the museum's curator, Julia Benites Arriola. She immediately began to tell us about the rich history of the home and its historic relevance. She showed us that the walls are sturdily constructed with twenty-three inches of adobe, and that some of the furnishings were actually donated by descendants of some the home's original residents. When asked if the house was haunted, she responded with, "Yes, some people do believe that we have spirits." She continued by saying, "In fact, the lady that left here not ten minutes ago told me, '*There are spirits here.*'"

As the reports go, several volunteers of the Sosa-Carrillo-Fremont House have heard footsteps in the main corridor of the home, a wide hallway that's known as a zaquan; typical of the Mexican style of architecture used in the home's design, which is tiled in Saltillo. It's a perfect sounding board for the disembodied steps of our ghostly forefathers.

Among the stately furnishings located in the main hallway is a very large mirror, so large that two or three people could stand side by side and see their complete reflections. Also sometimes visible in this mirror is the image of a woman dressed in period clothing, long since deceased. No one is sure whom the spirit belongs to, but the consensus is that she was a member of one of the families that lived here in the past, perhaps reluctant to leave this comfortable homestead.

Joining the other phantoms is the image of a man also dressed in clothing appropriate to the time period; he's often seen warming himself by the fireplace in the southernmost end of the home.

Although the expectations of Tucson's future may have required sacrifice of some of its past, it is clear that this part of our history will not be forgotten, and its colorful cast of characters plan to stay well past the last act.

Investigator's Comments

This house is such a pearl in the oyster of downtown Tucson. The Arizona Historical Society has managed to maintain the feeling that this is a home, not just a sterile landmark. At any moment, one might expect to see members of its original pioneer family gathered around the dining table, or perhaps see children running about, kicking up dust and giggling. It is that sense of family and home that keeps the visitors coming back to say, "Hello," while the ghostly residents remain to welcome them at the hearth.

‡‡‡‡‡‡‡‡‡‡‡‡

Court Street Cemetery

In some cases, though, it is the neighborhood. We have noticed an abundance of paranormal activity originating from the downtown Tucson area, and have always chalked it up to the probability that it was directly related to the fact that downtown Tucson is the center of the city, and has been formally occupied

Dunbar/Spring neighborhood, built atop the old Court Street Cemetery.

longer than any other part of Tucson. Adjacent to downtown Tucson is a little area called the Dunbar/Spring neighborhood. A quaint, close-knit neighborhood filled with historic homes and eccentric people, it also happens to be built directly atop the old Court Street Cemetery. The Court Street Cemetery existed, officially, between 1875 and 1909 and occupied much of the sixteen-block area that is now the Dunbar/Spring neighborhood.

Bounded by Speedway, Main Street, Stone Avenue, and Second Street, the cemetery was declared abandoned in 1916, with the land being sold to a developer who began constructing houses as early as 1914. Now, the way it was supposed to pan out was that the 6,000 or so graves were to be moved to the newer, nicer Evergreen and Holy Hope cemeteries, where they would spend the rest of eternity interred within this peaceful and well-maintained acreage. However, residents were given a very short amount of time to move their deceased, and, most often, the cost to move the graves was entirely too prohibitive for the regular, working class folk of the day. As such, only a small percentage of the actual graves were moved. In fact, of the gravestones that exist in Evergreen Cemetery as a result of the Court Street Cemetery debacle, only a small percentage of those mark actual graves. That leaves several thousand graves unaccounted for, buried beneath the foundations of the homes and businesses in this neighborhood. Aside from the occasional grave being accidentally disinterred through weather or construction, the residents of this neighborhood seem to have accepted the circumstances as the cost of doing business, and regard their deceased neighbors with the utmost dignity and respect. Some residents claim to have seen the ghosts of these forgotten forefathers strolling about, while others have erected a shrine to honor their memory.

We were fortunate enough to be contacted by Belinda, a resident of the Dunbar/Spring neighborhood, who has reported a number of strange goings-on since moving in two years ago.

Belinda and Andrew work alongside a rambunctious spirit in this Dunbar/ Spring house.

Her property, built in 1920, is part of the neighborhood that has been built atop the Court Street Cemetery, and it appears that she may be sharing the space with some unseen neighbors. She first suspected that something was amiss when she and her business colleague Andrew were painting in the basement shortly after taking possession of the building. According to Andrew, "We were down there painting and we hear something across the floor like steps...and all the doors were locked," something that they confirmed after running up the steps to investigate, and finding no one there. We paid Belinda and Andrew a visit for a small, informal investigation. Even as we were doing our walk-through, the ghost decided to make its presence known in Belinda's office.

"I had a feeling of being really apprehensive all of a sudden," Belinda recalls, "and then the software [for the scanner] is not even open for scanning, but it started scanning and then the back door popped open." Taking a look at the back door, it would take a bit of heft to push the door open hard enough to sound the chime, which rules out the possibility of an airflow issue.

This particular ghost seems to like mucking about with the office equipment. Andrew recalls another experience that sent chills down his spine. "I kept hearing something open and close, open and close...I went back in [to the small computer area] and the disk drive was open, closed, open, closed." An unusual situation for any computer, but what makes this even more spine-tingling is the fact that there was no power to the computer at that time, making the reasoning of a computer malfunction a virtual impossibility.

Also included among the shenanigans are a shredder that begins shredding, even with no power source, and an automatic stapler that fancied a habit of rapid-fire stapling until a stern scolding from Belinda to the apparent ghost put an abrupt stop to it. Belinda and Andrew are slowly accepting that they are living and working alongside an unseen occupant and at least she doesn't have to put him on the payroll!

Investigator's Comments

What made this small investigation very interesting was that the EMF (electromagnetic field) detector never stopped flashing. This is significant because the **EMF detector** is the device used to detect the presence of electromagnetic energy, which is often present concurrently with paranormal activity. We have used the detector on numerous other investigations, and had it flash a lot, but never has it given such a steady, uninterrupted signal. According to popular accepted practice, the presence of EMF can validate claims of paranormal activity, since most paranormal activity is comprised of some manner of electromagnetic energy. There were no power lines in the immediate vicinity, and there were not many electrical devices to account for the constant EMF. Given the history of the neighborhood, I don't think it is much of a stretch to acknowledge the probability of a higher than average paranormal presence.

‡‡‡‡‡‡‡‡‡‡‡‡‡

The Ghost of Z Mansion

According to the website for Z Mansion, it's "like stepping into the gilded age of America's Victorian tycoons." That may be an understatement. Located at 288 North Church Avenue, Z Mansion is a stunning reminder of the opulence that is a hallmark of the late 1800s. Built in 1898 by Charles Wright, the mansion has passed through the hands of several notable owners including the Zellwegers (from which the home derives

Z Mansion.

its name), Margaret Carmichael (co-owner of famed racehorse Secretariat), and Jay Pinkerton Murray (heir to the Pinkerton tobacco fortune) before becoming the home of noted author Thomas Langdon Hill, his wife Emmeline, and their seven children. Rumor has it that this home may have permanent occupants of the ethereal kind, as well.

We paid a visit to Z Mansion to get the scoop on the ghostly goings-on and were treated to a tour by sixteen-year-old Tiffer, who explained his view on the paranormal clearly at the outset. "I do tend to believe in ghosts...I don't really think this place is haunted." He explained that there are reports of the home being haunted, and there has even been a sensitive in the home who detected the spirit of someone by the name of William Thomas Harvey (whose portrait was hanging on a nearby wall at the time). Inconveniently, though, William Thomas Harvey made his residence in Maine and never lived in this particular home; an inconsistency which, by his own admission, lends itself to Tiffer's skepticism, although he also admits that "sometimes the place just feels weird."

One story that seems to support the theory that there are unseen residents inside of Z Mansion originates from the home's previous owners. According to the story, they witnessed the image of a woman, dressed in Victorian clothing, on the landing of the staircase. This image seemed to be validated on a subsequent trip to the Arizona Historical Society. When the homeowners were shown images of women who may have been associated with the home, they both pointed to the same picture, identifying its subject as the woman who was seen on the staircase. The woman in that photo was none other than Mrs. Charles Wright, wife of the home's original owner.

In spite of this experience, the jury is still out on whether the spirit of Mrs. Wright or any other ghosts remain at Z Mansion. According to Tiffer, "If anything, they are happy ghosts 'cause we are a happy family...or maybe we just scared all of them away!"

As well as being the home of the Hill family, Z Mansion is also available on a limited basis for weddings and parties, and would

The landing where the ghostly Victorian lady was seen at Z Mansion.

certainly be a gorgeous backdrop to anyone's special occasion. Perhaps if you are lucky, you may just have a few extra ghosts… er…guests at your wedding.

Investigator's Comments

The idea that this house may be haunted makes it, in my opinion, the best house on the block. Here you have a big, happy family who regularly open their home to host all manner of gatherings, making it their business to make sure you are having the time of your life against the gorgeous backdrop their home provides. This is a perfect example of "not all haunted houses are scary." If there is a ghost hanging around, who could blame them for wanting to blend in with the joyful chaos?

Residual Hauntings?

Kids See the Darnedest Things

It's beginning to surprise me to find out exactly how many reports of activity stem from my very own neighborhood. Such is the case with Robin and her family. Robin contacted us with such a great sense of urgency that we would have been irretrievably remiss in our duties not to follow up. Robin lives in an immaculate and unassuming apartment at Broadway Boulevard and Harrison Road. As we have discussed earlier, since most people picture haunted houses as old, gothic mansions that are well over a hundred years old, apartments are generally overlooked as viable settings for paranormal activity. Having lived in a haunted apartment, let me assure you that this is not the case.

††††††††††††††††

Robin starts off by explaining that the paranormal activity began when her son, daughter-in-law, and granddaughter were living in an apartment on the south side of town. The concern was that her three-year-old granddaughter began making references to people and things to which she had no previous exposure. The subject matter was also decidedly inappropriate for most adults, let alone a toddler. At the same time, she also began mentioning her new "friends" who, at one point, she announced were going into the bedroom to "have sex" and that everyone should "shhhh." Now, some people might read this and think, "Right...sounds like her parents need to be a little more careful around the kids," but having spoken to them, I feel quite confident that they are not the type of people to speak so irresponsibly around a young child. The granddaughter has mentioned both a man and woman, both of whom come

99

to "visit" her. At one point, the child was running around the apartment looking for her "baby," a game that is not uncommon for a three-year-old. What *IS* uncommon is the child explaining that she is looking for a baby who had died, a baby whose name was difficult for her to pronounce ("Macaya...") but that she knew meant "gift of God," and further explaining that the mother lived in a town called "McPrizen" and grew oranges, but because all the oranges died, they had to move.

Now, the Internet is a wonderful thing for researching such information and based on just those few odd details, I discovered that long ago there was a town called McPherson – now part of Orange, California – whose main trade was orange growing and that suffered two terrible freezes, once in 1912 and again in 1937, that caused devastating damage to the orange-growing industry. Although the words are not identical, it is not such a great stretch that a young child with limited linguistic capability should misunderstand or mispronounce it. What also strikes me as odd is that this town dates back to 1886, but has long since been absorbed by the surrounding community. As if that weren't unusual enough, the meaning of the baby's name – gift of God – perfectly describes the name Maceo...the name that she was having such difficulty pronouncing.

Now, all of this can be argued back and forth regarding its validity, but honestly, what are the odds that a child can weave such a story from whole cloth, relating such obscure yet verifiable details that most average adults wouldn't have without an intimate knowledge of the subject matter. While this does not provide irrefutable evidence of paranormal activity, it definitely creates justification for further investigation.

On the somewhat dubious advice of another paranormal investigating group, Robin's son and daughter-in-law abandoned all of their belongings and moved from their very active home into Robin's apartment, hopeful that they had left the madness behind. But a chilling statement from Robin's granddaughter stunted that hope as she informed her mother that her "friends" would be visiting her that night. This prompted Robin to contact us.

As is our custom, we arrived to investigate late in the evening and began with our usual walkthrough. Since the apartment was relatively small, we both chose to draw the floor plan and make notations. Although this apartment was small, it was definitely not without its share of unexplainable occurrences. We completed our walkthrough and began to get the low-down on the goings-on, and immediately we took notice that both of our maps had a remarkable number of hits. Of the seven or eight notations on our maps (indicating any number of odd sensations), at least five of those were exact matches. Even as we sat discussing the activity, a bedroom door slammed shut of its own volition.

Robin began to explain in exhaustive detail all that was occurring on a daily basis. The rest of the family began to notice little things – tiny voices whispering in their ears, hearing their names called when alone – but it's the young child who appears to be acting as a liaison between the living and the dead. The child's mother, Liza, described some of the statements coming through her such as "It's too late for us now, Mommy. Our dreams are flushed down the toilet."

Oftentimes, Liza will be watching her daughter playing contentedly only to see her turn away and stare off with a faraway gaze and whisper, "You're so pretty." The child has described the woman as having pale white skin and long dark hair. One evening while getting into her car, Liza was terrified as she looked into the rearview mirror only to see the reflection of a woman's face staring back at her. Without hesitation, Liza ran back to the apartment and refused to venture out again that night. Shortly after that incident, her daughter told her that wherever she goes, the woman follows her because she is too afraid of "the scary man."

Robin's accounting of the events went on to describe another spirit that seemed to be so frightening…*it was even frightening the other ghosts*. She described feeling very intimidated and afraid to be alone, especially when she tried to fall asleep at night. "As soon as I close my eyes I hear him…'you're a very beautiful woman.'" Not the least bit flattered by this statement Robin continues, "It was like he was saying, 'I can have you whenever I want you.'"

As frightening as it is to hear a phantom voice whispering not-so-sweet nothings in your ear, it is surpassed in shock value exponentially by that same disembodied voice waking you from your scarce slumber with angry, bellowing screams. Hearing just that sound, Robin bolted upright in her bed, flushed and with a rapid heartbeat, expecting to find a violent scene unfolding before her eyes. What she did find was just the opposite. As she attempted to regain her composure, her husband slept soundly in the bed...no sign whatsoever that he heard anything. Still hearing the angry yelling, she tentatively crept down her hallway towards the source of the noise — just behind the bedroom door where her son had been sleeping. Sure that she would find her panicked son having awoken from a bad dream, she threw the door wide open to find him sound asleep, blissfully unaware. Now, for anyone who has experienced anything similar to this, it will be quite easy to recall the overwhelming feeling of terror mixed with complete isolation at the discovery that there is no one available to share the burden of your fear. The experience is solely yours to endure, without the benefit of another conscious soul to dilute the intensity of the panic. It's as though the situation is calculated and premeditated in an effort for your tormentor to get you alone in the dark in a scary place and to dig into the most primal, visceral terror our bodies and minds can create. It's intimidation in its meanest, rawest form, and it preys on the tired, empty, fearful people who have become its unwilling housemates.

After our initial investigation, we scheduled another visit to follow up on the activity. We decided to go in with an uninvolved third party, Kat, who is a self-proclaimed sensitive. We have been very frank in our views regarding psychics and sensitives, but because of her **psychometric sensitivity**, *which is an ability to glean information and impressions by touching an affected object*, we thought it would be interesting to hear her input and see if she could replicate our findings.

Having no prior knowledge of any of the events, she carefully and methodically walked through the home, gently

Kat places her hands on the wall and senses an unkind presence.

placing her hand on the exposed surfaces and tracing her fingers along each counter, and wall, and door. She was immediately attracted to the second bedroom (the original source of the angry screaming). She lingered in a corner for a very long time, placing the palms of her hands against the back wall. We had been wandering in and out of the different rooms, taking photos and videos, when she rather quietly asked if we could take a photo in that corner. As I reached for the camera, I notice the EMF detector was emitting a solid red glow – beyond a flicker or a flashing – and registered the highest reading possible on this particular model. She said, "It's right here in this corner."

A check on the other side of the wall showed a humidifier placed low to the ground, and something resembling set dressing from a science fiction movie, compliments of the ghost-hunting group that had ordered the full scale evacuation, both of which were not positioned in such a way to correspond with what Kat was describing and what the detector was detecting. Kat calmly but insistently explained, "A woman was abused here — badly." Once she completed her entire walkthrough, she went on to describe that there is a man who is older, and this woman was much younger, and that he beat her severely. She further explained that she was getting a strange, inexplicable connection between that situation and the main bathroom, but she could not pinpoint the source of the connection, or why the bathroom gave her any sensation at all. Patrick and I exchanged surprised glances and pulled out our notes from the previous visit. Our strongest impressions and our biggest hits were in that bedroom and the nearby bathroom. Furthermore, the EMF spikes from the previous investigation did not even come close to the intensity of the one we registered in the exact location Kat was focusing on. This paranormal activity is the real deal – case closed.

Investigator's comments

While the source of the activity is now apparent, the investigation remains open and ongoing. The family feels some sense of validation that they are not losing their minds, but that does little to lessen the fear. The activity is caused by energy that cannot be stopped, so the goal has now become less about "what is going on, and how do I get rid of it?" and transitioned into "how do I deal with it without tearing my family apart?"

‡‡‡‡‡‡‡‡‡‡‡‡

Ghost Ranch

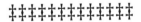

This next story, from my friend Ron, originates at a guest ranch immediately south of Tucson. Ron explains that he and his wife were hired as caretakers for the property, and as such they were permitted to park their RV on the property to serve as their living quarters. The owners of the property suggested that they park the vehicle in a pleasant, sheltered clearing that provided a great deal of sunshine. What made it very unusual was the fact that, no matter how warm the rest of the property got (and in

Arizona, that can well exceed 100 degrees), this location was always cold, and unless you have lived in Arizona, you may not fully comprehend that NOTHING ever gets "cold" during nine months of the year.

Not really giving it too much additional thought, they moved in and made themselves comfortable. One night, well after midnight, they were both awakened by the sound of the television turning itself on. Ron told me that he assumed it was one of the four cats they had sharing the space with them that had pressed its pudgy cat body against the remote and turned it on. Naturally, he groggily wandered out of his bedroom, turned off the television, and returned to bed. Not long after falling back to sleep, they were both awakened once again by the sound of the blaring television. This time, much less amused, he meandered to the television, turned it off, and hid the remote in a drawer.

For a third time that night, Ron and his wife were awakened from their precious slumber, only this time it was not just the television that had turned itself on, but also the microwave had powered itself up and was merrily nuking itself with that familiar microwave hum. According to Ron, they were never able to explain the cause of the eerie power surge, but it never happened again.

Another very bizarre incident that he recalled occurred during the filming of a motion picture on the property. The cast and crew were busily filming an outdoor scene when, much to everyone's chagrin, the sprinkler system burst forth with an unexpected rain shower. Given the high voltage of the situation, the movie folks were rather displeased and, as you might expect, Ron and the property owner ran like chickens with their heads cut off to stop the sprinklers. Arriving at the control box for the irrigation system, both Ron and the owner were a little thrown to find that not only was there no irrigation scheduled at that time, but that, according to the control panel, no irrigation was even occurring. The only way they were able to stop the sprinkler system was to kill power completely.

During their years there, they had come to terms with the activity, and had even given the "ghost" a pet name. In an odd coincidence, their next caretaking job led them to another guest ranch in southern Utah. Once they had gotten settled, the owner of this ranch pulled them aside to tell them not to be worried, but they had received several reports, over time, of paranormal activity and had come to accept the idea that a "ghost" was occupying their main dining room. The owner went on to humorously describe some of the stories that had taken place there, but Ron and his wife were both taken aback to learn the name they had given the ghost...it was the same name as the one they had just left behind.

Investigator's Comments

Now, as the reader, you don't have the benefit of knowing some of the storytellers personally, as we do. That being said, Ron is just about as straight an arrow as one would find. He is witty and loves a good laugh, but is not the type of person to weave a story like this from whole cloth. What he describes does not involve any type of apparition or haunting, so that leads me to think that it's the result of some convoluted poltergeist activity. Obviously there is a great deal of misdirected energy on the ranch, although it doesn't seem as though it originates from any one person as much as the land itself. I will reiterate again that there are no hard and fast rules about paranormal activity, only generally accepted categories. It would not be too farfetched to postulate that anything able to generate energy could also generate the activity. Most importantly, Ron is neither crazy nor insane, and this is a perfect example of the garden-variety paranormal activity that happens a lot more often than anyone realizes, or likes to think about at great length.

Tales of Another Kind

The Pacifier Thief

Patrick

Many ghost stories include the movement of objects. As we covered in the Introduction, the Big Three of activity segregates this type of occurrence to the poltergeist, which isn't a spirit at all. When looking at activity in a ghost story as a whole event, it's easy to lump all of the occurrences that take place into the same category or attribute them to the same source. This is not always the case, and as the next story will demonstrate, types of activity are not mutually exclusive. This story involves a mother and her small infant, the names of whom have been omitted for privacy.

✝✝✝✝✝✝✝✝✝✝✝✝✝✝✝

The family lived in a house on 22nd Street and Swan Road; the infant slept in her crib in the baby's room. Things started out in a fairly standard way: baby would go down for a nap, contentedly sucking on her pacifier. In fairly short order, however, the baby began to cry much more often than normal. Each time her mother went to check on the girl, her pacifier would be out of the baby's mouth and jettisoned across the crib.

This wasn't particularly alarming given that it's not unusual for babies to spit out or lose their pacifiers only to have them roll their way to the far reaches of the crib. If things had stayed that way, it would have merely been written off as exactly that. As it was, things were not so simple.

After days of these pacifier losses and retrievals, the pacifier in question began making its way out of the crib. Babies can certainly spit out a pacifier, which then rolls out into the crib and then through the open slats and onto the floor, with nothing strange about it. Again, that would have been fine had that been where it stopped, but given this is a ghost story and not a baby who spits out her pacifier story, you know that was not in the cards.

The mother began finding the pacifier at varying distances from the crib, eventually making it all the way to the other end of the room. Again, it's somewhat possible that the child had an arm that could make Curt Schilling blush, but finding a pacifier at the other end of the room stretches the credibility of "normal occurrence" to uncomfortable bounds. It's also unlikely that a newborn would have such an ability. Still, had it stopped there, one could conceivably write it off as "baby with impressive throwing arm, headed for professional sports," but of course, it did not.

It was nighttime and the baby was screaming, so her mother got up to go see what was the matter (and to retrieve the pacifier in all likelihood). What she found was much less routine. As she entered the hallway, she was confronted with the image of a teenager standing in the hallway wearing glasses. He was described as "geeky" according to whatever measures such things were judged over twenty-five years ago. As she moved closer, the figure disappeared and she made her way to the baby's room. Upon entering, she could not find the pacifier anywhere. She scoured the room and came up empty, eventually giving up and purchasing a new pacifier for the baby.

Days went by and, while the geek-ghost did not reappear, neither did the pacifier. It wasn't until several weeks had passed that the mother found the pacifier on the highest shelf of her husband's model-making room. Even if the baby had a bionic arm and a laser sight, it's impossible that she could have managed to throw the pacifier through several walls and across the house to land on the shelf of a model room.

So did the figure of the bespectacled geek snatch the baby's pacifier and "spirit" it away to the highest-reaching shelf of a room across the house, or was it some manner of diversion therapy for the baby to let go of her dependence on the pacifier? When you look at the details individually, it was probably neither.

Investigator's comments

The knee-jerk reaction when reading the above tale is to package the two odd occurrences together and assume they are the same, or if you are a skeptic, to assume that it was a prank being played by a human agent. I discard that explanation if only because in all of the times this happened, no such agent was ever discovered and frankly it would be really cruel and unsavory if it were true.

When you look at the situation with the eye of experience and knowledge of the generally accepted Big Three, you find that while the two events may be tenuously related, they are not at all the same phenomena and may have no causal link between them.

Clearly, the geek figure seems to be part of a haunting phenomenon, an image recorded in space and time. As covered earlier, the presence of clothing, glasses, and distinct features point to the culprit not being a spirit as eyeglasses and a button-up typically do not have souls to be represented on an apparition. In this case, the image was seen only once and its behavior was non-distinct, but it still falls directly into the haunting category given the aforementioned clothing.

When looking at the movement of the pacifier, clearly it's some manner of poltergeist activity. Again, as referenced previously, the poltergeist is more likely the product of a living individual's unleashed psychokinetic energy than a spirit manipulating objects. This means that someone in the household found themselves over-stressed and released that stress in a paranormal form. Usually, when this sort of thing happens, it's focused around an adolescent going through puberty and a high stress level, but it's certainly not exclusive to that age bracket.

In this instance, it would appear that the mother would be the most likely agent to be generating the poltergeist activity. The stress of childbirth combined with the added responsibilities of childcare could have manifested itself in the form of object manipulation. It's odd that the outcome of such stress relief would result in more work and ostensibly more stress for the parent, but that is sort of the point of uncontrolled energy—it does what it does.

It's also possible that the infant herself was generating the energy, perhaps in a bid for more attention from her mother, but there are few, if any, cases documented in which poltergeist activity is believed to be generated from a baby. But it's still a possibility, especially when considered next to the haunting activity that seemed to be running concurrently with the poltergeist activity.

As mentioned above, the presence of one type of activity does not preclude the presence of another. Sometimes the two work separately and have nothing at all to do with each other and other times the stress of one exacerbates the other. In this case, the child may have been seeing the haunting phenomena occurring in front of her and responded with some sort of psychokinetic lash out. Or, it could have been the mom who was stressed and overwhelmed and releasing that stress unconsciously. Either way, it is highly doubtful that our geek took the pacifier from the baby much in the same way that a character on a DVD playing on the TV isn't likely to take a bone away from the family dog. There is paranormal, and then there is just silly.

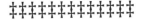

Maybe He Just Wanted Some Coffee

Katie

A common theme that we have mentioned when harvesting ghost stories is that if someone has one ghost story, they generally have a few. Such is the case with my friend Andrea. She was so helpful to us in sharing one of her ghost stories in *Scare-Izona* that I thought I would try asking her if she had any more. She did not disappoint. This story takes place in her current home – a repurposed Quonset hut – in central Tucson.

"One night, a little over a year ago, I was back in the

The kitchen where Andrea encountered the transparent man.

bedroom going through paperwork and I suddenly realized I had to go do something. I came around the corner and he was literally right where you are standing!" Andrea remembered. "My first thought was, 'Oh my GOD, there's a MAN in my KITCHEN!'...I came around the corner and I just stopped dead in my tracks and I was just looking at him. He had brown eyes, brown hair...I was in total shock...it happened so quickly...I was standing there looking

RIGHT at him…I remember looking down at what he was wearing and I remember he had a flannel, long-sleeved plaid shirt on, long khaki pants, and boots, and I remember thinking, 'Who dresses like that in Tucson?'… I just stood there and I'm looking at his clothes and I realized I could see *RIGHT THROUGH HIM*…"

Once it dawned on her that it was not a living man standing in her kitchen, she ran like lightning out of her kitchen and into the backyard where her boyfriend, Corey, was working in the shed. "Right when I realized there wasn't a man in my kitchen I was just like — I just ran, you know. I had to tell someone immediately…I was tripping on these stupid big shoes…Corey was back here and I started screaming 'Oh my GOD, babe, I just saw a ghost!' There was NOTHING in the shed, and I look to the right and there's this big cardboard box that he was going through, and in the box was nothing but this one book, and what is the title? *Paranormal.*"

Investigator's comments

This has all the attributes of a typical haunting. She was able to recall with perfect clarity exactly what this man was wearing. I think her story is particularly interesting because she actually paused long enough to look directly into his eyes, look him up and down, and commit his appearance to memory. Even though, based on common belief, he probably was completely unaware of her, it's still amazing that she had the intestinal fortitude to remain still for as long as she did. She has only seen the man one time, but she continues to sense someone in her kitchen with her when she is otherwise alone.

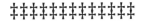

Ghost in the Mirror

Writing a book about ghosts makes one a bit shameless when it comes to soliciting stories. In a recent example, I was getting a much-needed haircut by my girl, Shannon, when the topic of haunted houses came up. "Do you know where Cathy Street is?" Shannon asked. "The house I grew up in there was haunted."

Evidently, according to a so-called sensitive, the house was being haunted by the spirit of a 14-year-old girl. "She was jealous of me," said Shannon, who was also a teenager at the time. One incident that Shannon recalled occurred late one night. Her parents were asleep and she was awake, watching a movie. All of a sudden, the vertical blinds, specifically the slats on either end of the blinds, started to shake violently, and the volume on the television turned itself up to the point where it almost woke her parents.

She even saw the ghost. "I saw her reflection in the mirror; I could see a glow behind me," she said, referring to a hallway mirror that she passed frequently. On one occasion, she passed by the mirror and it exploded off of the wall, showering her and the floor with bits of glass.

Shannon has no idea of the origin of the spirit, or any activities – disclosed or otherwise – that occurred in the house that might offer an explanation of the reported activity. Since the house has changed ownership, Shannon is also not sure if the activity continues, stating simply, "She didn't follow me."

Investigator's comments

This is another good example of the correlation between poltergeist activity and the phenomena of hauntings and apparitions. Given that Shannon was a teenager at the time, it certainly follows suit that the stress of living in a house with an insanely jealous ghost might unleash a few stray psychokinetic vibes.

Tucson's Workplace Ghosts

I Scream

O f all the landmark establishments in Tucson, perhaps the sweetest one is Austin's Ice Cream. Opened in its original location at 2920 East Broadway in 1959, it has been serving its famous selection of tempting confections for almost half a century, delighting the taste buds of generations of Tucsonans. It also seems that Austin's has, allegedly, attracted a different kind of patron — *the ghostly kind*.

Having recently moved from its original location to its new home across from Park Place Mall, it appears that the mischievous ghost may have followed. One former employee (who asked not to be identified) describes feeling a lot of "vibes" in the place, although she never actually saw anything.

"I helped the owner 'chase' a figure through the building once. We were closing the restaurant and had locked the front doors when the owner thought she saw a man in the back near the kitchen... she motioned for me to go through one side of the kitchen to 'head him off' as she approached from the other side. Just before we met in the middle, I got the coldest sensation and was covered in goose bumps from head to toe. It was only then that the owner realized that the man we were trying to catch was actually a ghost."

That wasn't the only experience she recalls. "Once I found a coffee cup broken into hundreds of pieces as if it had been thrown with force onto the floor. The thing that makes this interesting is that it was in an office that had been locked all night. I was the last one out and the first one in the next morning. The cup could not have just fallen off the desk because it was in the middle of the floor with the pieces spreading out."

In addition to those experiences, other employees recall tales of entire racks of pots and pans being knocked onto the floor with no corporeal influence, and objects in the kitchen moving around of their own accord, including the door to the walk-in cooler swinging open on its own.

No one is sure exactly who the playful spirit is that is running amok behind the scenes at Austin's, but it has been speculated that it's the original owner, Merrill Austin, keeping watch over the place and continuing to make his authoritative presence known. In any case, I would have to say that the ice cream is not the ONLY chilling thing about Austin's.

Investigator's comments

I think my first question would be, "Exactly where in the job description is the requirement to chase unseen marauders with intent to capture?" Of course, my second question would be, "Where do I apply?" Nevertheless, as we have seen and heard before, this follows the pattern of an apparition rather than a haunting. The idea that an owner has unfinished business to attend to is not beyond the realm of possibility, and the accounts, like others we have discussed, do not describe seeing distinguishing details of any kind. What is also interesting is the frequency with which apparitions occur simultaneously with poltergeist activity. The accepted theory of poltergeist activity suggests that it is the result of misdirected psychokinetic energy of a living person. Would it not also stand to reason that an apparition – who, by paranormal definition, has sentient capabilities – could also have a propensity towards poltergeist activity? Although there is no formal, scientific data upon which to base this theory, if poltergeist activity manifests as the result of unmanaged stress, it could easily be postulated that the stress of being dead, stuck in between the physical and the spiritual plane, and unable to communicate your discontent of the situation might just be enough to smash a few coffee cups here and there.

Tom's Fine Furniture – the home of the ghostly old lady.

The Ghost of Tom's Furniture

Located at 3402 East Grant Road is Tom's Fine Furniture. Consisting of two houses joined in the center, Tom's Fine Furniture is filled with gently used yet affordable furniture for all tastes. It also happens to be the home of at least one ghost. Originally built as two separate buildings in 1965, the homes were briefly occupied as residences before being joined together as one larger building that would first become the home of the popular Tia Elena restaurant before becoming Tom's Fine Furniture.

According to Terry Hogsett, who now manages the new location of Tom's Fine Furniture at Pima Street and Craycroft Road, there is definitely an unseen presence in the building: "It was just before closing...I saw a shadowy figure walk by and I thought someone else was in the store." Not surprisingly, he was the only person in the store at the time—but he was not the first person to report seeing *her* and probably will not be the last.

According to Terry, people who worked in the building when it was Tia Elena's frequently reported seeing the ghost of an older woman milling about in the kitchen. Terry also mentioned that, during the Tia Elena years, there has been at least one report of customers serving as an audience to paranormal pranks...as they watched two hanging plants begin to spin around above them, completely of their own accord.

Investigator's Comments

According to local lore, before the houses were joined together, an occupant of one of the homes – not coincidentally, an older woman – committed suicide inside the building. Now, that is complete hearsay and we have no way of substantiating that claim, but it certainly lends itself to the reports of the ghost of an older woman being seen for decades inside this otherwise unremarkable property.

‡‡‡‡‡‡‡‡‡‡‡

Phantom of the Wooden Nickel

Located at 1908 South Country Club Road, the building that houses the Wooden Nickel tavern has been a popular neighborhood watering hole since as far back as 1947 when it was the Polish American Club, and according to employees and patrons, some customers may still be hanging around long after their "closing time."

Reports of ghostly activity in the Wooden Nickel flow as freely as a freshly tapped keg, but these are definitely not inebriated ramblings. According to co-owner Joey, "I don't believe in ghosts, but I gotta tell ya...I DO hear the noises." Bartender Cecilia agrees. "We do hear all kinds of noises."

The Wooden Nickel Tavern, where more than one kind of spirit is on tap.

The noises in question happen all the time and consist mainly of heavy footsteps, although the activity isn't just limited to noises. "There have been a lot of people who see *him* walking into the kitchen or bathroom," explains Joey. Cecelia recalled a time when she was alone in the bar with a friend when her friend asked, "Who's that guy?" after seeing someone walk into a part of the building cordoned off for remodeling. Cecelia reminded her that there was nobody else in the building and her friend insisted, "I JUST SAW HIM WALK IN!"

118

Inside the Wooden Nickel Tavern, footsteps are heard and apparitions are seen well past happy hour.

On more than one occasion, Joey and Cecelia have been opening the bar and heard noises that went beyond just footsteps. Cecelia describes one of those times. "It was literally like someone was moving stuff around and walking. You can hear somebody walking...you just don't see anything."

Nobody is sure why the activity is occurring or who the culprit may be. However, that information appears to reveal itself on a video taken with Cecelia's camera phone. "As I was trying to take a picture, I kept getting this weird flash." At the same time, another person's camera phone stopped working completely and urged Cecelia to record it with her phone. "We took the video and this is what we got," she said. The video is astounding. With no source of reflection, there appears to be the figure of a man, standing in a column of light, right in front of the bar. His features are faint but visible, he looks to the right and then to the left. Of course, no one was actually there when the video was taken. One patron saw the video and said, "That looks like Smitty!" Smitty was a regular patron of the tavern until his passing, and now, perhaps, he is still hanging around.

Whoever or whatever is causing the commotion at the Wooden Nickel may be a mystery, but one thing that isn't is the friendly service and outstanding food. Joey even recalls his father bringing him to the tavern when he was a child. I asked him if he remembers anything strange happening to him, to which he replied, "I just remember the hamburgers were good!"

Investigator's comments

This actually fits the model of a haunting almost to a T. The patterns of activity are repetitive and the reports are consistent with each other. When the ghost is seen, he appears just as someone living would appear: fully articulated, with clothing and shoes. If this were an apparition, he would most likely appear as a shadow, and he may even try to communicate. When you pair this with the belief that the activity is being caused by a frequent patron of the bar, it completes the pattern. Here you have someone who probably had great times and great friends in this Cheers-like pub setting and he most certainly could have left an emotional print on the place. More commonly, this type of activity is related back to horrifying emotional events, but the key word here is "emotional." The emotions do not have to be bad to be strong. In the short time that we spent with the people at this Tavern, it's easy to see why anyone would want to stay just a little bit longer.

They Just Won't Leave

It would appear that Cecelia is no stranger to paranormal activity. As it turns out, she seems to have an abundance of that going on in her world. "Everyone's *seen* them," she said, referring to the three ghosts that apparently take up residence in her home of the last eighteen years. Evidently, the activity is so abundant that it has become hard to get people to spend any great length of time there. "I have had people housesit who won't housesit anymore."

According to Cecelia, there is a man and two children who are frequently seen and heard at this 1950s-era home at Park Avenue and Irvington Road. On one ill-fated house-sitting occasion, her niece, who had previously declared her patent disbelief in any such supernatural goings-on by saying, "Your house isn't haunted! I'm not scared!" phoned her in a panic to tell her that the kitchen cabinet kept opening on its own, to which Cecelia replied, "It's just the ghost." Unable to maintain her cool exterior, Cecelia's niece put the phone down long enough to go into the next room, but when she returned, not just one but ALL of the cabinets were opened, bringing to a close that particular house-sitting endeavor.

Witnessing this activity is certainly not limited to just house-sitters. Every member of the family has experienced the ghosts. Cecelia recalls a time when they had just gotten new furniture. "We were vacuuming the carpets, and you could see footprints in the carpet."

Her son insists on leaving a light on in his bedroom because, Cecelia explains, "The kids bother my kids a lot." She describes the children to appear as dark shadows, but the man is clearly defined with a goatee and a baseball cap. These ghosts are certainly not going to give Casper a run for his money in the "friendly-ghost" department anytime soon. "The guy, once in a while I'll fight with him in my sleep and I'll wake up scratched," explains Cecelia.

Among the ghostly pranks that she has fallen victim to, Cecelia describes things that disappear and reappear. "A bracelet disappeared. It was my favorite bracelet, and I couldn't find it and couldn't find it...a year later it was laying there as if I had just taken it off and put it there." Apparently that is not the only thing that has gone missing. "The kids are more playful, they hide my keys." On one occasion, she was forced to send someone else to go retrieve her kids from school because she had already been running late, and her keys had vanished from their normal resting place. "After I'd been looking for a half hour for my keys, I found them stuck in the vent."

It seems that these "extras" are what allowed Cecilia and her husband to acquire the property for a song two decades ago. Their sentiment at the time was, "Yeah. Ghosts. Whatever." Although now they can agree that the ghosts are definitely active, Cecelia's family has grown tolerant of the extra occupants, but that sentiment is definitely not shared by the previous owners. "The people who lived there before us, the girl is still in therapy...we didn't know it was that serious for her...they won't have anything to do with the house!"

Investigator's comments

By now we have pretty well established the different categories of paranormal activity, and this tale has examples of all three, which is pretty common. The one interesting subsection of paranormal phenomena that we haven't discussed before this story is what has become known as "stigmatized properties." *A **stigmatized property** is basically any property that is linked with a scandal that can hurt the resale value of the home*. Sometimes, the scandals are nothing more than highly-publicized affairs or white-collar crimes. More often, though, these scandals involve homicide, suicide, and – both as a by-product and a separate category – haunting phenomena. Just to give you an example of how common this is — if I am standing in front of my house, I can look east to the end of the street that, when it was still undeveloped land, was the scene of a grizzly, gang-land style drug-related triple murder, or I can look to the west towards the house that, just a few years ago, was the scene of a murder-suicide, and I live in a GOOD neighborhood. Nevertheless, the imprint that this type of trauma leaves on a property and in a neighborhood is what causes a property to be referred to as stigmatized. The upside to this is that these properties can often be acquired for thousands below market value, because, well, who would want to live in THAT house?

Now, before all you house-hunters get bugged out about buying a stigmatized property, you can rest assured. Realtors are obligated by disclosure laws to tell you everything they know about a property—good and bad. That doesn't necessarily mean you won't end up with a friendly ghost or two, but it does mean that with a little research and the right questions you can be comfortable in the knowledge that you won't end up with a nasty little Ronny Defeo-esque surprise. Of course, if you are LOOKING for that type of a house, you need only ask. There's one in every neighborhood.

Anne & Bobby's Ghostly Adventures

Tales of Old Tucson

When Columbia Pictures chose a parcel of land owned by Pima County to film the motion picture *Arizona*, it not only modernized Hollywood movie-making standards, but it also branded Tucson as the go-to location for westerns because of the authenticity of its surroundings. The original movie set was constructed in 1939 and, although the studio lay dormant for several years after, it eventually became so popular with movie makers that it was dubbed "Hollywood in the Desert." The list of actors that have graced this film studio reads like a who's who of the silver screen. William Holden, Bing Crosby, Jimmy Stewart, and Ronald Reagan have all filmed there, not to mention John Wayne and, later, Clint Eastwood, just to name a few.

With each movie that was filmed, the set grew as new buildings were constructed to meet the needs of the current production. "Rio Bravo" (1959) added a saloon, bank building, and doctor's office; and "MCLINTOCK!" (1963) added the McLintock Hotel. In 1970, the studio expanded again when the production of "Rio Lobo" added a cantina, a granite-lined creek, a jail, and Philip's ranch house. The rich history of Old Tucson Studios compounded with the completion of each feature length production, keeping its present well-connected to its past. Located "12 miles and a hundred years from town," Old Tucson kept the Wild West alive, memorializing it in film for generations to come. I remember the feeling of walking down those dirt streets for the very first time as a young child, thinking, "Wow, movie stars have been here!" The history was alive and present.

Sadly, on April 25, 1995, a devastating fire destroyed almost half of the landmark's original structures, claiming the original soundstage, the entire Kansas Street filming region, and many historically significant props including the wardrobe from "Little House on the Prairie." I can recall standing in front of my television, eyes wide and mouth agape, as I (along with the rest of the city) watched the live footage of the studio engulfed in flames. In that moment, the heart of this tough, old cowboy stopped beating, and we began to grieve for the loss of this wonderful connection to our history. No longer could we look into his eyes and see the past. We would now have to be content to remember through photos and stories.

Of course, Old Tucson has rebuilt and continues to operate as a fun, family-oriented western-themed amusement park. During the month of October, Old Tucson's Halloween show, Nightfall, is especially popular. The western-themed streets and buildings transform into the town by the same name, and it becomes inhabited by escapees of the Goulliard Asylum who wreak havoc

This sign outside of the Iron Door Mine at Old Tucson describes more than just the ride.

and mayhem in the normally peaceful community. But does this seasonal façade of lunacy belie a much scarier presence within Old Tucson's walls? Turns out there could be some real ghosts hanging around.

According to one former employee named Anne, activity occurs all over the park, although two locations that see frequent paranormal activity are the Grand Palace Saloon and the adjacent Rosa's Cantina. What type of activity? Anne stated simply, "Rosa calling my name, asking me to help her." Rosa is the name employees have given to the female spirit they frequently encounter, and evidently she can be quite insistent. "I heard my name, but it was drawn out, like 'Aaaaaane.' I'm like, 'okay, what?' and I'm counting down the till and it's between shows and I hear it again…'Aaaaaane,' so I closed it, locked it, and left."

That was not the last time that Anne heard Rosa calling her name. Convinced she was having some sort of post-partum

Grand Palace, Old Tucson.

126

Rosa's Cantina at Old Tucson, where employees (and Katie) had their hair pulled by the ghost.

issue after returning to work too soon after the birth of her daughter, she shrugged it off as hormones. A few days later, she had another experience. "I got lunch, I'm at Rosa's Cantina, and I hear it again, 'Aaaaane, come help me!'" Thinking it was a coworker, she walked towards a small room in the Grand Palace and she heard it again, "Aaaaane, come help me!" She quickened her step, but shuddered when she arrived at the location of the voice—and was greeted by an empty room. Interestingly, I may have had my own run-in with the ghost while taking photos for the book. Recalling something that I experienced that I thought was odd, I asked Anne if she had ever felt the sensation that something had touched her, or brushed past her at Old Tucson, explaining that I felt something odd. She laughed a little and said to me, "I will tell you where it touched you. It's not a hard feeling, it's underneath your hair"

Inside the Grand Palace (connected to Rosa's Cantina), where Anne heard her name being called by the phantom voice.

and she made a motion that showed the type of hair-pulling that was so frequent.

She described my experience spot-on.

Across the park, at the Storyteller Theater, there are also reports of activity. According to Anne, you can hear a woman screaming "like she's being murdered." The activity surrounding the Storyteller Theater appears to be much less friendly—and far more sinister than Rosa—and may actually be responsible for some potentially dangerous mishaps during the Nightfall show of 1999. Anne's husband, Bobby, was a stunt performer at Nightfall that year and he explained that another stunt performer was doing a routine safety check of the harness equipment (which is kept under lock and key to prevent any such tampering, and its use being strictly supervised) and made an interesting discovery: "There were pieces of popcorn inside the wheels!" Had this gone undiscovered prior to the show, the popcorn could have easily lodged inside the mechanism, causing serious injury. The ghost may have found this tom-foolery to be funny, but Bobby certainly didn't. "We never do that to each other. It's dangerous."

Investigator's Comments

As with so many of Tucson's haunted landmarks, it appears that there are all types of paranormal activity happening concurrently. Nobody is certain of the source of the activity within Old Tucson, but just about everyone agrees that it does indeed exist. Some rumors mention a worker who died of a heart attack on the property and others suggest that the land once housed a long since forgotten insane asylum. Add to that the probability that Native Americans occupied that land centuries before the theme park, and you have the perfect recipe for the paranormal.

✠✠✠✠✠✠✠✠✠✠✠✠

Nothing's Wrong... Everything's Okay.

Patrick

In the beginning of the book, we detailed the various and sundry categories of activity and how they usually manifest. This next pair of locations will show that activity doesn't always play by the rules. They will also demonstrate the same pattern that has already appeared earlier in this book, that paranormal activity is not at all like lightning—it doesn't just strike once. The variety of activity in the next stories is enormously varied and runs the gamut of experience, even mixing and matching in a way that is typically not seen and with a consistency the likes of which are generally unheard. At the end it goes to show how nothing is certain, no one is exempt, and it can happen to a perfectly normal family.

The first location is a house on Mission and Ajo Streets on the southwest side of town. The house was inhabited by Anne and Bobby, both of whom also shared their Old Tucson experiences, and their children, son DJ, and daughters Tiffany and Sammy. As a family, they are no different than any other you are likely to encounter: loving, supportive, and normal. The house itself, aside from being old, a trait fairly typical of houses in Tucson, also appeared to be perfectly normal. Of course, as the saying goes, appearances can be deceiving.

The first time anything strange happened in the house, it found Tiffany in the bedroom she shared with her younger sister Sammy. They slept in a bunk bed with Tiffany taking the top bunk like any older sister would. Sometime in the night, Tiffany was stirred awake by movement in the room and when she looked over the side of the bed, she saw a girl standing there. Tiffany took the girl to be Sammy initially and just looked at her quizzically. The girl said, "Don't worry, I won't leave you." Then, as if to put a lie to the statement, the girl left the room.

Tiffany, obviously weirded out by her sister getting up out of bed and saying something cryptic only to then leave the room in the middle of the night, waited a moment before she did anything. When she moved again, it was to check the bunk below and she was shocked to find Sammy perfectly asleep in her bed.

Tiffany told her story the next day, describing the girl in details as specific as the dress she wore and the distinct face she could make out in the dark, and was met with a certain level of skepticism. That skepticism would not last, however, as the girl was apparently not satisfied with her one cameo into this family's lives.

Her next appearance would happen a short time later as Anne encountered the girl in the hallway. Anne felt like she was being stared at and looked up to see the girl she would also mistake for Sammy to be standing in the hallway. Reflexively Anne asked the girl she thought was her youngest daughter what was wrong. The girl replied, "Nothing's wrong."

Given the lateness of the hour and Anne's unwillingness to play games with a daughter out of bed, she found her patience slipping and she said, "What? What? What? Go back to bed." Again, the girl said, "Nothing's wrong, everything's okay." Again Anne told her to go to bed and the girl appeared to do so.

The next morning, Anne confronted her daughter about the incident and told her in no uncertain terms that she could not be getting out of bed like that. Sammy vehemently denied ever having gotten out of bed, an assertion corroborated by Tiffany, who would have noticed had her sister gotten up and left the room. Then it dawned on Anne, who said, "Oh, I just saw what she saw."

Rounding out the trifecta of speaking engagements for the little girl, she again appeared to Anne in the hallway. This time, Anne and DJ were in the living room watching TV. The girls were in Anne's room due to the quarantine of one of their cats who had recently had kittens in the girls' room. So, being temporarily evicted in light of the kitty annex their room had become, the girls were asleep in Anne's room at the end of the hall with the door closed.

As Anne and DJ sat watching TV, the non-incarcerated dog and cats ran down the hallway suddenly. Anne got up to investigate the sudden animal migration and found the girl standing at the bedroom door. At first, Anne again mistook the girl for Sammy and told her to go back to bed. The girl said, "Nothing's wrong." Anne realized that she was again seeing the mystery girl, and got a closer look. In the hallway, Anne could now discern more details than previously gleaned about the girl's appearance. She wore a light blue dress with a floral print. She was beautiful, with white skin the color and look of porcelain. Also, she had no top lip of any kind.

Alarmed, Anne turned around and called DJ into the hallway to see. He took his time getting there, not particularly wanting to get out of his comfortable spot, and when he got to the hallway, there was nothing there but Anne and the pets.

These three appearances of the little girl would be enough for most stories, and would comprise the sum total of experiences for a given location but even when not speaking, the little girl would appear many more times. The further appearances of the girl would be as simple as Tiffany seeing someone go into her bedroom only to find that no one was in there. The rest of the family reports having seen figures go in and out of bedrooms from time to time.

The girl's activities were not limited to simply wandering the house assuring whoever would listen that she was okay; she also had a fancy for photography. Taking pictures of the house, Anne found some of the pictures inhabited not only by the little girl, but also a woman with a large nose. The pictures featuring these two interlopers were taken ten minutes apart and attempts to print said pictures always ended in a printer error. While showing a family friend the photos, Anne and her friend heard the sound of a child giggling. Sadly, the computer with the pictures on the hard drive was stolen and the pictures lost forever.

Most stories would end there, the exploits of the little girl more than enough for most families and most locations. Again, this is not most stories. As the family moved to a new house in a new part of town, the 22nd Street and Swan Road area to be precise, they hoped that they had left their paranormal activity behind them. As is sometimes the case, this was not meant to be. No quarter was given either, if they were hoping for a lighter sentence this time. The second house proved to be much more prolific in its variety of activity as well as its rate of occurrence.

There is not as clear a narrative for the second house as there was for the first. The first house almost seemed to have some manner of storyline running through it with the appearances of the little girl. The second house holds more of a collection of activity and events than a cohesive story of sightings and sounds.

This house, too, is a much more daunting prospect to live in. Whereas the last house offered up spectral little girls and orbs, this house seems to deliver a much more disruptive experience. This can be as minor, albeit annoying, as the toilet flushing on its own during the night, but it can also be much bigger.

One such instance found DJ in the living room. He had fallen asleep watching TV and woke up to find the stereo on. He thought it was the TV at first and reached for the remote to turn down the TV and found that the TV was already off. The music, Reba McEntire's "I'll Hold You Forever," was piping out of the stereo speakers. DJ tried to turn down the stereo volume only to find it all the way down already. It occurred to him that the radio shouldn't be playing a country song as it had been tuned to a rock station, so he ejected the disc on the CD player to find it empty. As it turns out, the Reba CD had been missing for two years. This would not be the last time the CD would play. Over the course of their stay in the house, the stereo has come on in the night several times and always plays the missing CD.

The missing CD is not the only item to disappear, either. Over the years the family at large have found items missing and subsequently replaced by other items. It has gotten so bad as to lead to friends of the kids being accused of theft, as was the case with a missing digital camera. A search of the child's room and duffle bag and one ruined friendship led to the conclusion that the child had not lifted said item. Just as mysteriously, replacement items are found, such as a doll and a library book from the Scottsdale Library. Certainly there seems to be little equity in the returned items when compared to the taken ones, but at least whatever is doing this is courteous enough to leave *something.*

Despite this apparent conscientiousness on the part of the "entity," Anne and Bobby have found themselves refraining from buying many high-dollar or nice items because of the overriding fear that the item will disappear and be replaced with a gum wrapper or a book on Eastern European landscaping. Obviously, such a concern is something of a confound when you are trying to go about your life.

Sometimes, the something left behind is not even an item at all, but a residual sound. Rather than being comforting, this can add insult to injury as in the case involving the stolen computer. After its disappearance, it could still be heard turning on and off despite the computer's abject lack of existing in the space.

Then, there's the cabinets and drawers in the kitchen... which are loathe to stay put. This is an exceedingly common experience and happens three to four times a week and has gone on for three years. The activity started only three weeks after the family moved in. Anne will wake up in the morning and come into the kitchen to find the cabinet doors and drawers standing open and the chairs stacked asymmetrically on the table. The first time this happened, she was so convinced that Bobby had done it as a prank she called him at lunch and demanded he come home. When he got home, he was as stunned and bewildered as she was, and indeed the chair stacking seemed impossible to align properly, especially under the cover of early morning darkness and some semblance of quiet. The activity has continued weekly and has become a part of their typical routine to fix.

Not all of the activity has been as relatively benign, though. Some of it actually crosses over into violent and disturbing. Bobby, in particular, has had several run-ins with this. From the time he moved in, it started on him. At first it was simple; the door would often open when he was in the shower and he would hear a voice ask, "Are you in there Robbie?" While that voice was unsettling but generally harmless, the next escalation became much more disturbing. Bobby would get out of the shower and find his body covered in angry red scratches. These scratches did not hurt or feel like anything in particular, they just showed up during the shower and obviously weren't there before.

This sort of business escalated into objects being moved around to violent results. The first of these found a gun safe, not a light object by any stretch of the imagination, falling off a shelf and hitting Bobby in the shoulder. At the time, he was not doing anything that would cause the safe to fall. Obviously heavy objects don't generally throw themselves off a shelf on a whim, and Bobby was alarmed. Anne, too, got her share of such behavior when one of the wily kitchen cabinets swung open and cracked her in the head while she was making dinner.

One incident didn't involve any sort of object, but rather some kind of unseen force. Youngest daughter Sammy was walking down the hall one day and thought she saw someone behind her. As she was turning around to see who it was, she was hit from behind and pushed into the wall. There was no one in the hall but her and she was left with a nasty purple bruise.

The family dog was not immune to this activity, either. One day they found the dog missing and all the doors were secured tightly. Bobby went to investigate and found the dog outside, whimpering at the back door. Add to this the spectral sounds of a dog scratching the door outside of DJ's room—despite the absence of a dog to produce the scratches, and it seems that no member of the family is immune to ghostly shenanigans.

Adding to the list of shenanigans, the vacuum turns itself on and off even while securely plugged in. In order for operation of the appliance to resume, the user must tell it loudly to turn on again. It is the sort of behavior one finds in science fiction movies...but much more annoying. Further, the family will hear knocking sounds on the doors when no one is there as well as similar knocking on the walls and cabinets. Crosses on walls will fall down and containers of holy water in the house will turn over and dump their sacred contents all over the floor. Clocks tend to stop and the roof will rattle.

In the face of all this seeming disparate activity, DJ decided to do a bit of investigating on his own. He set up a camera in front of his parents' mirror and told the ghost out loud to come out and play. This is never a particularly good idea when dealing with such a cantankerous "entity" as evidenced by the results. When he returned, he found the tripod bent. The tape itself showed the camera shaking, the door in the room banging, and the camera bouncing.

Again, most stories would stop here, but this house has the determination of a late night infomercial huckster proclaiming, "But wait there's more!" In addition to physical objects being moved around, figures and voices seem to also roam the house as well. The foremost example of a figure sighting was actually experienced by an uncle visiting the house. The uncle was sitting on a couch in the living room that was situated close to the kitchen and saw a man who "looked like he was really, really pissed." He was dressed in a checkered flannel shirt like he had just gotten off work. The uncle exclaimed, "What the hell is this?" and got up to "whup somebody." Of course upon mobilizing, the figure disappeared and the uncle was left in the room alone.

Apparent residual haunting-type figures aren't the only ones traipsing around the house, however. Every night for the entire tenure of their stay, the family has witnessed silhouettes of figures walking past the windows. Now, obviously the first thought for this sort of activity is that it's simply people walking by outside; however, in this case, the figures are *in front* of the window shades as opposed to behind. These figures occur every night at the same time and quick trips outside to see who was walking there revealed that the answer was, in fact, no one. In addition to these fact-finding missions, there is a motion sensor outside that would come on if there was actually anyone out there, and there are no footsteps of any kind to be heard. Another such incident of this sort involved

Anne's other son who was visiting. He was walking down the hall and saw a figure going into Anne's bedroom. He followed it into the bedroom to find Bobby in the room alone. No one at all had come in.

A figure is also seen walking into the kitchen in front of the refrigerator from time to time. In this case, the figure is the standard dark apparition. It moves methodically from the entryway to the front of the refrigerator. It's an odd example of an apparent apparition performing repetitive actions. Just because it's an apparition as opposed to a haunting doesn't mean it doesn't have its habits.

Sounds are also prevalent; bangs, voices, and footsteps. Tiffany was in her room at one point and heard footsteps inside the room with her. Obviously alarmed by this given there was no one in the room, she fled to find Anne. The two came back to investigate, but predictably, there was nothing out of the ordinary in the room.

Upon returning from a trip to the store, Anne approached the door with her hands full of grocery bags. She tried to open the door and found it would not budge. Already a difficult feat with grocery bags in her hands, the door was being especially stubborn. After what seemed like an eternity in the hot Arizona sun, the door finally swung open and she prepared to enter the house. She stopped short, however, when she came face to face with a man standing there. As Anne puts it, "I freaked and dropped the damn eggs."

DJ, in particular, seems to have a volatile relationship with whatever is going on in the house. In addition to once having to leave his room after getting dizzy and nauseated while thinking of the activity, he also had a more personal tussle with one of the house's extra inhabitants. DJ and the dog were in his room when the dog started growling. DJ heard a voice from outside the room say, "Come out and play." DJ didn't bite that time, but he would hear the voice again.

The next time he heard the voice it was as he was sleeping. DJ awoke to the voice calling to him saying, "I need some help with this," and "Hey, you want to come help me?" Thinking it was his dad, DJ got up and followed the voice. As he looked around the house, following the voice, it again said, "Come out and play." He eventually made his way to the back room of the house and the voice came from behind him this time: "Hey, I am over here!" DJ turned around and found no one behind him. DJ was fairly freaked out, describing the moment as, "I felt like I was going to piss myself." He proceeded to make his way back to his bed and pulled the covers over his head.

As we stated previously, this family has had quite a run of luck with their houses. Whether it's good or bad luck is open for interpretation, but there is no doubt that they have lived in two of the most haunted places in the city.

Investigator's comments

With a collection of activity this prolific, it's difficult to know where to begin. There seems to be representation of pretty much every major activity type over and over again. Even more interesting, however, is the tendency for these activity types to mix and match with each other. The notion that there are no hard and fast rules in the paranormal is certainly on display here.

The most troubling of all the activity is the apparent poltergeist activity that seems to consistently lead to injury. It sort of flies in the face of the idea that paranormal activity is generally safe. In these examples, it's hard to really explain the activity in the normal manner. None of the cases show a central figure or "contact" to be possibly perpetuating the activity. So the theory that the movement is caused by unconscious, unleashed psychokinetic energy is put to the test and comes up somewhat wanting. I'm inclined to believe that this sort of activity is indeed human-generated PK energy, but in this case I'm at a loss to explain it that way. Alternate explanations escape me since in none of the instances are there precipitating factors that may have made the objects move or appear to move by themselves. Certainly gusts of air from air-conditioning vents or swamp coolers can explain a cabinet swinging if it's open a little already, but you would be hard-pressed to find a gust of air-conditioning that could push a gun safe off a shelf—and if you could, I want that a/c unit in my apartment immediately. Any other force capable of dislodging such a heavy object would not go unnoticed by Bobby and would be easily noted. Likewise, Sammy being pushed into a wall is not something explained away by something like a burst of air. Perhaps she tripped as she was walking, but that is not an experience likely to be confused with being hit from behind and shoved into a wall.

What I am left with in the face of this is the notion that while a great deal, if not all, of poltergeist activity is caused by a human subject, there is room for the possibility that an apparition can manipulate objects in at least rudimentary ways. Of course, for that sort of business, you would have to have an apparition.

The second house, which is of course the site of all the apparent poltergeist activity, definitely seems to have at least one apparition running around. The dark shadowy figures that are seen in windows and going into bedrooms, down hallways, and in the kitchen definitely seem to behave the way the garden-variety apparition does. While the activities of the entity can be repetitive, there seems to be a rhyme and reason behind said activities.

The voices too seem to be attributed to some sort of sentient entity. They seem to have a goal and seem to want attention. Again they are repetitive in nature, but that may point to a persistent aim that the apparition has as opposed to belonging to a residual haunting. The sort of taunting quality the voices take on with DJ in particular is consistent at best with the mischievous activities like taking items and turning on Reba in the middle of the night, and at worst with the violent and disruptive acting out on other members of the family.

The missing items are not in and of themselves uncommon when dealing with an apparition, and cabinet doors opening and chair stacking are equally common. Again this points to at least some ability on the part of the apparition to be able to manipulate objects. In these cases, however, Anne does seem to be a consistent cast member and could conceivably be an agent of PK energy in those cases.

In the case of the first house and a good many of the sightings in the second house, the activity is mostly of the residual variety. Vocalization in the recorded images is not uncommon and the clothed figures in both cases behave in exclusively repetitive ways. It's tempting to assume that the little girl in House #1 was really trying to communicate with the family, but the presence of clothing and the fact that the things she said never really changed flies solidly in the face of such an assumption. Hauntings are often the most fanciful of the varieties of activity because they look like people. They seem to be more real than an ill-defined shape or shadow even though they are perhaps much less "real" in the cognitive sense of the word.

Without a personal investigation of the activity in question, it's impossible to say for certain what is causing all this activity and how "legitimate" the activity is; however, it has that telltale consistency and general theme that suggests the stories are true and legitimate. In speaking with the family, you are struck right away with the notion that not only are they very normal and not wont to tell fanciful stories, but also that they are reluctant to even share the stories. Like so many people who have had these sorts of experiences, they have had their share of being called crazy and their stories untrue. Nothing can be definitively concluded, but it's our opinion that based on the stories told and the manner in which they were confided, this activity is both legitimate and profound. There may be those out there who wish they lived in a haunted house and on that score one must really look at this particular case and ask himself really hard if he is maybe being a little more wistful than is terribly good for him.

3

Ghostly Pets

Of all the categories of ghost stories one hears when studying the paranormal, one of the lesser reported sort is animal activity. Many of the stories you tend to hear will have been diluted to the point that all of them involve either a mischievous little girl or an angry old man. If you took all the childhood tales that you were told and sifted through the ghostly culprits, you will find a preponderance of tales regarding mean old men and nice, helpful little girls. This is not always the case.

Although not as common, I would have to say that, if asked, I would be more willing to believe the majority of these animal stories than the cookie cutter ghost stories most of the time. One of the likely reasons that animal spirit stories take the back seat to Old Man Withers and Annabelle the Moppet is that they are less dramatic and scary. But the bigger reason is that whether animals have souls to become ghosts in the first place is a hotly debated item, especially amongst Christians of different denominations. I don't intend to weigh in on that particular debate, except to say that the number of animal stories you hear certainly suggests something more than a pile of skin and bones for our furry friends. The next few stories are about our dearly departed companions and the similarity between the stories can suggest a commonality that denotes truth.

‡‡‡‡‡‡‡‡‡‡‡‡‡

Patches the Kitty

When Michelle was younger, she and her brother got two kittens; one was named Piggy and the other was named Patches. Patches was Michelle's brother's kitten, but animals, especially cats, tend to pick their own friends regardless of their intended owner. Patches was no exception and formed a bond with Michelle right away that would prove to be the deepest bond with an animal she had ever experienced.

Patches followed Michelle around the house, slept nestled in her arms at night and even "talked" to her in a series of insistent meows. This went on for eleven years, every day and every night. Unfortunately, Patches was born with small kidneys and as she got older, the condition began to make things increasingly difficult for her and she started to lose weight. Eventually she got to a point where she no longer had the energy to eat and drink on her own.

Michelle, being in tune with her cat, knew that when she took her into the vet, her cat would not be able to live through the next day, so she did what any loving friend would. She made Patches as comfortable as possible, let her sit in her window, brought her food and water, helping her to eat and drink, and slept with her snuggled under her arm that night. The vet's news was as expected and Patches would continue to suffer without daily dialysis that would drastically impose on her quality of life. She was put to sleep that afternoon, with her friend sitting with her and giving her love until the end.

As one would expect, Michelle was devastated by the loss of her friend. Even now, the story is difficult for her to relive. But as these stories go, that afternoon at the vet's would not be the last time she would see Patches.

About two or three weeks after Patches' death, Michelle would start to see things out the corner of her eye. She would sit reading and see a flash of white run into the room from around the corner, keeping low to the ground. This startled her as it was

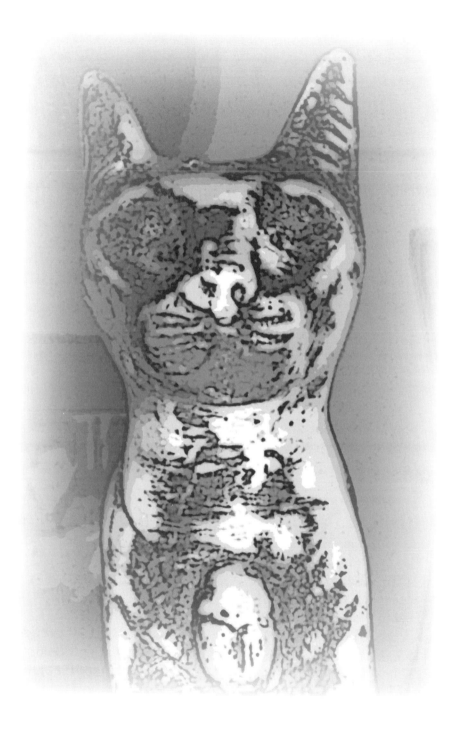

how Patches, a black and white cat, usually came in the room to see her. It was something she was used to, but not something she expected to see again. This sort of thing happened quite often for a number of months, and there was never a clear definition of a cat, just a shape moving in a familiar way. That too changed one afternoon.

Michelle was in the kitchen cooking when a cat walked in the room. She responded to the cat the way most of us do, in our particular form of baby talk or cute noises, but when she turned to look at her kitty, there was no kitty to be found. Piggy was still around so she thought to write it off as her cat wandering in and out, but when she went to look for Piggy she found her in her parents' bed across the house. These sorts of sightings continued for months and then quietly disappeared, but their presence was of great comfort to Michelle.

‡‡‡‡‡‡‡‡‡‡‡‡‡

Goldie's Ghost

The next story is a short one. Mila, who you'll remember from a previous story, had a dog named Goldie, a golden lab/weimaraner mix who had a habit of flinging herself into the sliding glass patio door when Mila and her family would get home. She would go from a standing position to flying through the air and, due to her size, land with enough impact to shake the house such that those returning home could hear it from outside on the other side of the house. This did not hurt her at all, but rather seemed to quite amuse her.

After Goldie passed, each member of Mila's family has reported a continuation of this behavior. Upon arriving home, they would be greeted by the sound of Goldie jumping against the door, regardless of the fact that there was no Goldie to do such a thing.

Goldie didn't stop there, though. Prior to a rearranging of the house and a switching of rooms, Mila would often feel something

144

get into bed with her in the same way Goldie used to, and a visible depression would be seen in the bed in the general shape of the animal. It stopped once rooms were switched, but for a long time before that, Mila felt comforted by her friend coming back to her.

✝✝✝✝✝✝✝✝✝✝✝✝✝

Rowdy the Poodle

Patrick

The final story is my own. When I was young, my grandparents got a toy poodle from relatives in Oregon. He was the brother of my aunt and uncle's two poodles who were named Ruff and Ready, so keeping with the alliteration, he was named Rowdy. From the time my grandparents got him, he was bonded with my grandpa. Poodles tend to latch on to and bond with one person and my grandpa was it. He would wipe his feet when he came in from going outside only for my grandpa. When it was time for Papa to come home from work, Rowdy would be there waiting for him, spinning little circles of joy for his best friend.

I was a child then and I grew attached to Rowdy. He loved me too, but Papa was his best friend. Still, he would come and spend the night at my house a lot and we had a fairly close bond as well. Eventually, and devastatingly, my grandpa had a heart attack and did not survive surgery. The family was brought to its knees by this and it remains one of the saddest moments in our history. Everyone was very close to my grandpa and he remains one of the greatest men I have ever had the pleasure of knowing.

My last words to my grandpa were that I would bring Rowdy to the hospital to see him after his surgery the next day because I knew he wanted to see him. When we got back from the hospital the next day, Rowdy was lying in front of the door and I got the impression from his down and sullen behavior that he knew that grandpa was gone.

Because of our bond, when everything was said and done, Rowdy came to live with us and was "my dog." He began wiping his feet for me and we had a strong unspoken bond, and I could often tell what he wanted before he would bark or scratch. He was there for me in perhaps my most difficult time emotionally, and I fully believed that he was my only friend at that time. He seemed very in tune with my emotional state and was always there to make me feel better. I feel no shame whatsoever in saying he was my best friend at the time and will always remain so. Even as I write this, I miss him deeply.

Rowdy was the runt of the litter and as such, had a hole in his heart. This is not very uncommon amongst small breeds like poodles, particularly the runts. There was little we could do; the vet told us that surgery had such a small success rate that it was more dangerous than not doing it. He was given about a year or so. That year saw Rowdy getting weaker and weaker. He would have seizures in which he would cough and convulse and we had to rub him and talk to him for them to stop. He was not in great pain and for most of the time the seizures were few and far between.

When I would come home, he showed his excitement by walking in a slow circle, no longer having the strength to dance, but wanting to show me he was excited anyway. One afternoon when I was a sophomore in high school, I heard him coughing from my parents' room. I was on the phone at the time and threw it down immediately. I knew the sound he made when he coughed and this was different. I knew he was dying. I ran in the room and scooped him into my arms and held him, telling him I loved him and that I didn't want him to go, but I knew there was no stopping it. I held him and looked into his eyes and saw the moment that he was no longer there. (Despite my refusal to take a stand on this earlier I submit that anyone who says an animal has no soul after seeing the moment of death is a fool. One minute Rowdy was there, the next he was gone.)

While I was glad to be there for him in his final moments, his death haunted me in my dreams. I had recurring nightmares where I would see him and go to pick him up and he would die again. This went on for years after his death. Obviously, it was a very sad time for me. Years went by and I found myself in a fair bit of personal emotional turmoil. This time, I was pretty much alone. I was somewhat estranged from my parents and my personal relationships were strained if not non-existent at the time. It was there in the depths of all of that, that my friend came back to help me.

At that time I slept in a water bed and it had a padded side board, intended to keep a person from rolling around on the waves and cracking his head open in the night. The bed was fairly low to the ground, and before his death, Rowdy could jump up into it, but would usually prefer to be lifted. So he would try to scratch at the padded part. His scratching was rhythmic in the way people knock three times. It was three quick scratches. One night, in the midst of my overblown emotional angst, I heard three scratches. Thinking I was obviously hearing things, I ignored it. It came again, this time harder and more insistent. Because of my nightmares I didn't dare look, I just kept my back turned to the side and tried to go to sleep. Eventually it stopped.

I dismissed it as a product of an overactive imagination in a haunted house and moved on. A few days later it happened again. Again, I tried to ignore it. This time, however, after about four scratch groups, I heard the sound of something jumping up into bed. The sound is distinct as it is the sound of scraping on the pad, and of the bottom of the pad hitting wood. Then I felt something walk across the bed and lay down at the small of my back. In a water bed, you can feel every movement so it was not something that would be imagined or misconstrued, and I felt the weight of a small body pressed against my back, the exact place Rowdy used to lay. I could also feel warmth there. I couldn't help but look so I remained in the same position but looked over my shoulder. I saw a poodle shaped lump there in the covers. I didn't dare try to touch it, but I knew it was Rowdy coming back to comfort me. I lay my head down and went to sleep and felt better. I knew that no matter what, my friend was always there for me, and that is a good feeling to have.

Investigator's Comments

The one thing that strikes me about the pet stories, my own included, is the consistency across the three stories. In all instances, the animals seemed to be doing the same repetitive behavior they displayed in life. Because of this, it's tempting to assign these cases to the residual haunting category and assume that animals have no souls, case closed. I think that sort of categorization would be a bit hasty.

It is worth noting, off the bat, that my take on this may be motivated by a very real desire for the spirits of animals to endure. Still, even given that, I feel like the nature of the activity itself points to a true apparition type situation. In all of the cases, the activity seemed to center around an emotional response or a specific activity. People come home, the walls bang and shake like they used to, someone is sad, the animal shows up to comfort them. The sort of physical representations like dents in the bed or a raised hump in the covers also shows more of a real presence than a residual haunting would afford. You add to that the fact that the repetitious behavior speaks more toward the natural inclination of animals more than the haunting activity, and I think you have a good case for an apparition.

4

Rumor Has It...

Katie

S ince the purpose of this book is to convince the general public that paranormal activity leans more towards the "normal" end of the spectrum (and, of course, to showcase all the ghostly goodness the Old Pueblo has to offer), we really want to give a shout out to a few places in Tucson that everyone has visited, but probably didn't realize were ALLEGEDLY haunted. While we weren't able to get them to freely admit they have had an inexplicable brush with the supernatural in these locations, enough people have circulated the stories that they bear repeating, so here it goes:

San Xavier Del Bac Mission – Built between 1783 and 1797, San Xavier is arguably the most stunning example of Mission architecture. The bright white building pops against the beiges and greens of the desert, and its formidable countenance beckons to travelers of I-19. According to legend, several spirits and specters have been seen within the Mission, including the image of an old priest walking through the church and a nun leading children into the church from a schoolhouse (which is said to have burned to the ground, killing everyone inside). Another popular bit of lore describes the image of a snake (in some stories, a cat) and the image of a mouse separated by the main doors of the mission. According to legend, if the snake catches the mouse, the end of the world is near.

El Tiradito, also known as the Wishing Shrine, dedicated to the memory of a sinner.

El Tiradito – Also known as the "wishing shrine," this memorial is located in the Barrio Viejo section of downtown Tucson, and is touted as the only shrine in the United States dedicated to the memory of a sinner. As the legend goes, Juan Oliveras worked for his father-in-law on a ranch outside of Tucson and fell in love with his own mother-in-law. When Juan's father-in-law caught them in the act of their adultery, he chased his son-in-law down with an ax and murdered him. Because Juan committed such a scandalous sin, the Catholic Church refused him burial in consecrated ground, and now his remains are said to be buried in the spot where he was murdered, underneath the shrine. Visitors to this monument place written prayers and heart's desires within the cracks of the shrine's walls, and light candles in remembrance of Juan and his crime of passion. It is said that if a candle remains lit through the night, the wish made when the candle was lit will come true. Some even claim that if you light a candle at dusk, you will catch a glimpse of Juan's heartbroken ghost.

‡‡‡‡‡‡‡‡‡‡‡‡‡

Sam Levitz Furniture – This story is fairly recent in that the activity started around 2000. According to reports, an employee was retrieving a piece of furniture from a rack, high above the warehouse, when he slipped and fell to his death. Since then, numerous employees have described seeing the image of this fellow, or heard footsteps, often in the wee hours of the morning. On a few occasions, large pieces of furniture have mysteriously dropped from the racks where the employee fell — when no one else was in the building.

Manning House.

The Manning House – Built in 1907 by Henry Trost, this massive banquet hall was originally home to Tucson mayor Levi Howell Manning and his family. Mr. Manning lived there until his death in 1935. There have been several rumored reports of paranormal activity, and it's believed that the ghost of Levi Manning's son Howell still roams the building.

‡‡‡‡‡‡‡‡‡‡‡‡

Copper Bell Bed and Breakfast – Located at the base of "A" Mountain, this imposing lava-stone building was constructed between 1907 and 1920. So much activity has been reported at this residence that it has been investigated several times

Copper Bell Bed and Breakfast.

152

by parapsychologist William Everist and the students in his parapsychology class at Pima Community College.

✠✠✠✠✠✠✠✠✠✠✠✠

Lakeside Park – According to legend, a young girl met an untimely and particularly unpleasant death inside of one of the park's drainage tunnels. It's her ghost that is allegedly seen walking around the area of the park where her body was discovered. Hers is not the only death that has been reported within the small park on Tucson's east side, and therefore may not be the only spirit causing a ruckus.

✠✠✠✠✠✠✠✠✠✠✠✠

El Charro Café Restaurant – This delightful restaurant has been in operation since 1922 and is the oldest Mexican restaurant in continuous operation by the same family, according to the

El Charro Café.

The historic Santa Rita Hotel.

The once luxurious Santa Rita Hotel now stands empty, except for the ghost of room 822.

restaurant's website. Not only is this restaurant considered to be the home of the chimichanga, it's also believed to be the home of a ghost or two. Many have whispered of alleged paranormal activity at the Court Street location that includes hearing one's name being called and the image of an old woman appearing.

‡‡‡‡‡‡‡‡‡‡‡‡

Santa Rita Hotel – Originally built in 1904, this Tucson landmark was a fixture for celebrities like Gregory Peck, Cary Grant, and Clark Gable and was a very happening hot spot during its heyday.

Evidently it's such a great place that at least one guest doesn't want to leave — even though the hotel has been closed for some time. According to reports, room 822 is believed to be haunted by a rather rambunctious spirit, although the identity of the ghost remains a mystery. Sadly, the location is now totally inaccessible to the general public, but it's rumored to be slated for conversion into condominiums. Get your deposit in early and maybe you can have the haunted condo!

Conclusion

As you can see, Tucson is one haunted town. From furniture stores and ice cream shops, to an entire community buried beneath a downtown neighborhood, ghosts are everywhere—and they aren't going away anytime soon (at least we hope not!). Honestly, this book only scratches the surface of Tucson's haunted legacy, due largely to the veil of secrecy that hangs over the entire topic of the paranormal. Tucsonans will happily tell their ghost stories, as long as they don't have to go on record as officially believing that they actually exist. I'm also willing to speculate that nowadays people aren't particularly interested in having THEIR home or business be labeled or stigmatized in any way that might affect its resale value. To these people I would like to say, "Embrace your ghosts!" It's illogical and impossible that any parcel of land NOT be the site of some event that may imprint itself on the delicate parchment of eternity, to be replayed for the lucky few that are both able and willing to acknowledge the activity. Not only that, I would like to think that the idea of people surviving in some capacity beyond death would be of great comfort to everyone, given that we are all rapidly propelling in that same direction. At any rate, the ghosts are here and THEY are certainly willing to make their collective presence known, even if everybody is just pretending they don't exist. I'm very thankful to the people who willingly participated in the collection of these stories, and I'm hopeful that everyone else will eventually come around.

Another interesting side note to compiling these tales is this: some of the locations in Tucson that are alleged to be haunted AREN'T! During the long and arduous research phase of this book, I contacted some locations in the downtown area that, according to numerous internet sites, are absolutely brimming with paranormal activity, but when I spoke to the owners and managers, none could recall even one incident that might remotely lend itself to the buildings in question being haunted. Even after I pointed out to the manager of one location that the establishment was, in fact, included on a local ghost tour that is in no way affiliated with our group, he explained that members of that group had come in and, based exclusively on their personal sensations, determined the location to be haunted. I imagine that makes for very interesting fodder for a tour group, but it's more than a little disappointing to learn that some of the ghost stories are completely unsubstantiated.

Hopefully, what this book has done is begin the process of changing the way that people view paranormal activity. Rather than seeing it as completely esoteric and incomprehensible (and exclusively the territory of wildly-gesticulating, self-proclaimed clairvoyant "knowers"), we would hope that society would begin to see it from our perspective and the perspectives of everyone currently embroiled in supernatural melodrama. It is completely normal. It *happens* every day...to everyday people. These encounters are only a small sampling of activity that occurs daily and on a worldwide basis. Having a ghost story or believing in the paranormal does not make you crazy, however, feeling like you can't tell anyone may slowly drive you insane.

If you are currently experiencing what you believe to be paranormal activity, or know of someone who is dealing with a similar situation, or just want to share your ghost story or ask a question, please feel free to contact us at our website: www.wailingbansidhe.com, or email us at info@wailingbansidhe.com.

Glossary

Apparition: The literal soul of a dead person. The apparition is one of the Big Three of haunting phenomena. Typically manifesting as a silhouette or shadow, the Apparition seems to have actual intelligence.

Crisis Apparition: The manifestation of someone recently deceased or in great peril, the crisis apparition usually involves people seeing a loved one suddenly, regardless of distance. It is generally believed this is a way of saying goodbye or calling for help.

Electromagnetic Field (EMF): Field of electromagnetic energy around a person or an object. Can be generated by any electronic device or power cords, but becomes significant when fields are found where they do not belong in a location alleged to have paranormal activity.

EMF Detector: Device that finds electromagnetic fields. A must have for any investigator.

Entity: Typically referring to an apparition, it's used interchangeably with any supposed agent of a haunting.

Extra-Sensory Perception (ESP): Term coined by J. B. Rine to refer to a constellation of paranormal abilities including: Telepathy, Clairvoyance, Remote Viewing, and Precognition.

Haunting: Usually referred to as a residual haunting, this is another of the Big Three. Thought to be a recording of an event on space and time, the Haunting is characterized by inanimate objects being represented along with human figures.

Paranormal: The prefix, "para" indicates something that is irregular, faulty, or operating outside the usual boundaries. So, "paranormal" refers to anything outside the realm and experiences that we consider normal.

Poltergeist: The last of the Big Three, poltergeist is German for "noisy spirit" and is characterized by objects moving around the room. Common belief holds that this is not a ghost at all, but rather the unconscious efforts of a human agent through PK ability.

Psychokinesis (PK): What is more commonly known as telekinesis, this is the ability to manipulate objects with one's mind.

Psychometric Sensitivity: The ability purported by some psychics to gain images or information by touching an object.

Remote Viewing: A form of ESP in which a subject attempts to mentally see through another's eyes.

Stigmatized Property: Any property where a murder, suicide, or heinous crime has occurred. Reports of haunting phenomena fall into this category as well.

Vortex of Energy: Used often by psychics, this somewhat questionable designation denotes a mass of energy centering around one particular spot. Often times nothing but unsubstantiated hornswaggle.

References

www.arizonahistoricalsociety.org

www.elcharrocafe.com

www.manninghouse.com

www.oldtucson.com

www.tucsonweekly.com

www.zmansion.com